I love these old bears. All banged up from a lifetime of struggle. They live mostly on wits and lessons learned, each face with a thousand stories.

DENNIS COMPAYRE

WRITTEN BY *Dennis Compayre* | PHOTOGRAPHS BY *Andrew Bagley*

Waiting for Dancer.

Waiting for Dancer.

© 2015 Published by
TECSHOTS
PO Box 676086
Rancho Santa Fe, California, USA
92067
tecshots.com

All rights reserved. Published 2015

9 8 7 6 5 4 3 2 1

waitingfordancer.com

Text copyright © Dennis Compayre
Photographs copyright © Andrew Bazeley
Art and illustrative lettering © Kal Barteski
Photographs on pages 15, 28, 41, 43, 45, 154 courtesy
of Kal Barteski.

No part of this book may be reproduced or transmitted
in any form or by any means, including digital alteration,
without permission in writing from the publisher, except by
a reviewer who may quote brief passages in a review.

No bears were harmed in the making of this book.

First printing
Printed and bound in Canada by
Friesens Corporation
One Printers Way
Altona, Manitoba, CANADA R0G 0B0

ISBN: 978-0-9963399-0-2

What is man without the beasts?
If all the beasts were gone,
man would die from
great loneliness of spirit,
for whatever happens to the
beasts also happens to the man —
All things are connected.

Chief Seattle
DUWAMISH TRIBE

table of contents

FOREWORD BY KAL BARTESKI **15**
INTRODUCTION BY ANDREW BAZELEY **19**
WAITING FOR DANCER **29**
PHOTOGRAPHS **76**
ACKNOWLEDGEMENTS **155**

I've learned that storytelling is everything and that everything in the wild has a story to tell.

— DENNIS COMPAYRE

As a strong north wind brought heavy snow flurries, this mom had just finished nursing her cubs and decided to check us out. /ANDREW BAZELEY

Andrew Bazeley

Wildlife photographer Andrew Bazeley has traveled the world capturing images of brown bears in Alaska, lions on the African savanna, and the great white sharks of Mexico and South Africa, but since 2008 his passion has been the polar bears of subarctic Canada. Captivated by their regal beauty and ability survive under the harshest conditions, he travels regularly to Churchill, Manitoba, using his lens to document the Earth's largest land predator. He seeks innovative and daring techniques for capturing wildlife imagery, aiming to reveal the grace and wonder of the animal kingdom in ways never seen before. A native of Australia, Andrew resides in San Diego, California. His portfolio of wildlife images from around the globe can be found at tecshots.com.

Dennis Compayre

A native of Churchill, Manitoba, Dennis Compayre was a pioneer in the movement to introduce the world to polar bears in the wild and is regarded as one of the most experienced guides on Hudson Bay, home to one of the Earth's largest polar bear populations. He was the visionary behind the Polar Bear Cam, bringing real-time footage of the bears in their natural habitat to computer screens around the world. Using his established viewing techniques based on learned bear behavior, he works as a guide and consultant for film crews, still photographers, and naturalists who visit the region each year to witness the majestic creatures on land and ice. After more than three decades and thirty thousand hours spent observing bears in their natural habitat, his passion for these noble animals has not diminished. While he divides his time between Winnipeg and Baker Lake, Nunavut, he still considers Churchill home.

You cannot underestimate the intelligence of polar bears. The more I am around them, the more I am convinced that their ingenuity will see them through the hardest of times.

D.C.

foreword

BEAR SEASON in Churchill, Manitoba, happens in October and November each year. It turns a sleepy subarctic town into a flurry of tourists, seasonal workers, conservation officers, and polar bears. *The ice is coming.* The energy is electric. Churchill is on the path of the annual polar bear migration. The bears come to wait for sea ice so they can leave on the frozen ocean to feed.

It's not unusual to see a bear walking on the main street or to hear cracker shells as they are ushered out.

I am an artist who paints polar bears. I ended up in Churchill, like everyone you will find there, to see bears. I didn't bring a camera. I'm drawn to the things you can't capture on film. I am fascinated by bears — their mechanics, characteristics, noises, glances, feelings—the invisible power.

After an exhilarating day of bear watching, there is nothing better than warming up and recounting memories over rounds of beer. It is common to see large groups of smiling folks—faces red from the wind and the weather, winter gear peeled half away and an assortment of mittens, toques, and scarves piled all about their table. They are brought together by an appreciation of these beautiful beasts.

There's something magical about seeing a polar bear in the wild. No matter where you're from, it is a spiritual privilege to see the world's largest predators lounging in the winter sun, breastfeeding their young, investigating interesting smells, or going about their regular itinerary.

It was there, in a dimly lit Legion Hall on the night of a wicked blizzard that I met Dennis Compayre and Andrew Bazeley.

An unlikely duo with riveting stories and tall beers, I believe their admiration for polars bears brought them together. Maybe they see their own struggles within this exceptional creature. I have witnessed the resiliency and creativity—of bears and also men. They have shown me unexpected kindness and friendship. We have enjoyed rambling conversations about the complicated world of polar bears—from the business side to the curious ways of conservation—from local, global, and personal perspectives. They have taught me so much about polar bears, but also about the human spirit.

I did not expect to find meaningful friendships in the weathered characters I met in an old bar in a small northern town but I am humbly grateful.

It has been a pleasure to help bring together Andrew's photographs and Dennis' stories. I hope you enjoy this collection. I am so fond of these two old bears.

KAL BARTESKI

introduction

I first visited Churchill in 2008, hooked by the marketing hype from the tour groups saying that the polar bear was on the fast track to extinction. So I booked a week on the Great White Bear Tundra Lodge for my wife, Susan, and myself. We didn't actually see too many bears because freeze-up was early that year and there were only a few stragglers left. It was -4° F (-20° C) with a hard-blowing wind from the north and near whiteout conditions. The few bears we did see were heading out to work in the brutal winter conditions they thrive in and that was nice to witness.

On that first trip with Susan, all of the bear viewing and photography was done from the relative comfort of tourist buggies. I pretty quickly decided that the tundra buggies were not for me—too many people jostling for position, too high off the ground, everything just too damned choreographed. So, on the stopover in Churchill on the way out, I hit the pavement and started asking around. I was looking for a guide who could get me up close and on the ground with the bears. And that's how I found Dennis. I didn't actually meet him—I just received an email address—but it was a start. The one that fast-tracked me into the polar bear world.

When I was hunting for a guide on that first trip to Churchill, I ran into the mayor, Mike Spence. Mike and his brother Morris operate Wat'chee Lodge, a rough-and-tumble old army building sitting right in the area where the mother polar bears den and have cubs. The location is incredible for taking pictures and Wat'chee is always filled to the brim with as many as twenty hardy photographers. It just so happened that a slot had come open and Mike offered it to me. So, in late February of 2009, I was headed off to Churchill for the second time in just three months. The Wat'chee experience was incredible—watching and shooting mothers leaving the dens with their three-month-old cubs. But it was cold—as cold as -94° F (-70° C) at times.

This time, on the stopover in Churchill, I finally met Dennis in the bar of the Seaport Hotel, a place the locals affectionately call "The Dark Side." A big Paul Bunyan with a deep gravelly voice, Dennis and I had a connection right from the start. I knew when I returned for bear season later that year that things with Dennis would go well— and they did.

Now, eight trips to Churchill later, Dennis and I continue to work together during bear season. Along the way, we have had some pretty incredible adventures and photographed some pretty incredible bears and bear behavior.

On my first trip to Wat'chee Lodge I began to appreciate the incredibly difficult and arduous journey that a mother polar bear goes through to raise and train one or two, and occasionally three, cubs. In November, about the time that the rest of the polar bears are heading out onto the sea ice to start their winter of gorging on seal, the expectant mother is heading in the other direction towards the denning area that lies about thirty miles (fifty kilometers) away. At this point, she hasn't eaten since she stepped off the melting sea ice five months earlier, in June. She'll find her old den, or if she is a first timer she will find an abandoned den, and she'll wait in it until the wind-driven snow covers it over. Once hidden, the mother to be will open a small breathing hole in the snow. She just stays in that den, growing one or two or maybe three cubs inside her until they are born right around Christmas. Remember, she hasn't eaten since June. Drinking milk rich in seal fat, the cubs quickly go from less than a pound to around fifteen pounds by the time mom opens up that breathing hole and lets them out to explore and exercise around the den in late February or early March. By now, the mother's fat reserves are pretty depleted and her milk is running out. She has to get those cubs strong enough to make the thirty-mile (fifty kilometer) trek to the frozen sea ice, where she can hunt and eat seal and make more milk. But she can only move the cubs about half a mile (one kilometer) before they tire and need to nurse, so if she works them hard they can move

IN MEMORIAM - SUSAN MARIE BAZELEY

about six miles (ten kilometers) a day. She is running on empty, her milk supply is pretty close to exhausted, she has cubs who are ravenous and often not so well-behaved, and she has one other major factor to deal with—wolves. A mother can protect one cub from one wolf but it is pretty hard to protect two, or certainly three, from a pack of wolves. Many cubs are lost on this journey, and it is an incredible testament to the fierce devotion of the mother that so many make it safely to the sea ice. This journey can take place as late as mid-March, which means the mother hasn't eaten for close to nine months.

The mother and cubs arrival on the ice in early spring coincides with the birth of tens of thousands of ringed seal pups. Breaking into the seal dens and feasting on seal pups is relatively easy compared to hunting adult seal, so this is a reasonably good feeding time for a mother bear. She is able to replenish her body and milk supply after nine months without seal. It's also a safer time for the cubs because the easy availability of seal pups means that the big males are less likely to try to kill and eat them. For the next year, mother's milk will be the cubs' only food. In their second year, the mother will let them eat a little seal to supplement the milk. So for two years, or until the mother goes into estrus again, she will keep the cubs by her side. She will have them hide and watch as she hunts seal, so that they learn that most important skill. She will teach them to swim, to climb out of the water onto the ice, to dry their fur by sliding in snow, how to spread their weight out when on thin ice, how to build a snow cave, and a whole host of other survival skills. And as they get older, she will let them wander into potentially dangerous situations—coming too close to a male bear, coming too close to humans, walking on thin ice—so that they learn by their mistakes. And then, when she figures that they can survive on their own, she will leave them to get pregnant and start the whole process over again.

Arguably, the mother polar bear has the toughest job of any animal on this planet—and she does that job with exceptional skill, poise, and grace. We use the polar bear to symbolize what's wrong with our planet—as the poster child for global warming—and this makes the bear appear weak and incompetent. Instead, we should venerate this most fearful apex predator and celebrate the mother polar bear for her fierce devotion to her cubs in the face of almost insurmountable odds. We should use her to symbolize just how damned tough a woman's job can be—and just how damned tough a woman can be—in a world where so many of the odds are stacked against her.

And so, I dedicate this book to the memory of my wife of thirty years, Susan, who lost her battle against the odds in April of 2014, but not before she had raised two cubs of her own and taught them how to survive in the world.

ANDREW BAZELEY

Polar bears can spar like this for days – and often do. Funny thing is, nobody ever gets hurt. Maybe an accidental spot of blood but not often. Doing this helps kill time while waiting for freeze-up and also helps them build strength and fighting skills that they will need while out on the ice – either to fight for food or for mates. /A.B.

My hometown on the edge

n teeters
of the wild.

D.C.

Growing up in a rough-and-tumble place like Churchill, there were way too many things to worry about.

—D.C.

growing up in Churchill

My hometown teeters on the edge of the wild. We are neither Arctic nor wooded nor fully in The Barrens, yet much of the flora and fauna found in those ecosystems sit at our doorstep. A rich marine environment flush with whale and seal, a vast array of migrating and nesting birds, and the wonder of the aurora borealis all contribute to a life closely shared with nature. We are known as "The Polar Bear Capital of the World." This amazing animal is the one we most identify with and, to a certain extent, have learned to coexist with. It wasn't always this way.

Growing up in a rough-and-tumble place like Churchill, there were way too many things to worry about. If it wasn't the searing cold, it was the feral dogs. If it wasn't the feral dogs, it was the fear of falling through the ice. If it wasn't the fear of falling through the ice and drowning, it was the damn bears. Polar bears were the main ingredient for my childhood nightmares.

The idea that polar bears were a threat to our well-being was constantly reinforced throughout my childhood. One of the first lessons taught in school was how to best survive a bear attack. Later, in my teen years, I understood why. More than a few friends had serious run-ins with bears that ended badly. Unlike today, polar bears were neither a major contributor to our economy nor were they perceived to be threatened by a wonky climate. No one was coming forward in their defense. Old Churchill was a mix of hunters and trappers, railroad men and dockworkers, and soldiers returning from the war who looked north to start anew. They had no room in their lives to ponder the wonders of the natural world—they were too busy trying to survive it. As a child, this community seldom gave a second chance to a bear that found itself caught amongst the snow-banked houses and icy streets. Change was hard coming.

Thankfully, one can't carry the full force of a childhood fear around forever, and my views towards the bears softened somewhat as I got older. In retrospect, a childhood living with these noble beasts could be frightening, but it brought with it a certain amount of excitement. There was danger in the air when in the dark of a long winter's night the alarm was raised because a bear was in town. Dad's rifle came out of the closet and was leaned against the wall by the door as the frenzied half-barks and howls from the dogs chained outside faded in and out with the wind. All of the lights were shut off so a bear couldn't see in but we could see out. In those days, houses were built close to the ground. With the snow piled up, a bear could walk right through the picture window. The thrill and trepidation twisted my stomach into knots.

I expect all small towns have things in common and things that set them apart. The Churchill of my youth certainly had things that made it different. I can't imagine any other town that could cause so much grief for a boy.

Geography didn't help. The Canadian Arctic is recognized when crossing the sixtieth parallel north—my town is located just before you hit the fifty-ninth. The boreal forest makes its last stand here giving way to the Great Barren Lands in the west and northwest. The Hudson Bay Lowlands run east along the coast for a while before taking a dogleg to the south. Churchill is the end of the line for anyone traveling by train, which is one of the very few ways to get here. All roads end about 185 miles (three hundred kilometers) south.

Our greatest feature, the reason for being here, is the always tempest and unforgiving Hudson Bay, a huge body of cold salt water that reaches past horizons from the north to the southeast. A large contributor to this northern sea is the Churchill River, a historic waterway that starts gathering itself far to the west before spilling its contents at our doorstep. The town sits amid this confusion of land and water, with buildings and homes built on frozen ground leveled with tons of gravel. No lawns or gardens. Geography wouldn't allow it. The town where I grew up wasn't pretty or quaint—it was hard and rough and cold—but an appreciation of one's surroundings comes much later in life. It may sound like my childhood was an overwhelming struggle. Yet there is value in struggle, and strength, if you choose to learn from it.

Summers were quick—mitts off mid-June, mitts on come September. It seems like it was always windy, always winter, with frost clinging to the inside walls around the door and windows. There was no plumbing in the house during the 1950s. A forty-five gallon drum to hold water sat beside the door with a thin sheet of ice to break for morning tea. The cranky oil furnace had a prominent place in the small house, keeping us warm from the knees up unless it decided to quit. When it did, the chill was felt immediately. The concern on Mom's face was a worry for us all. No amount of blankets would offer any comfort until Dad coaxed it back to life again and the muffled hiss of the flame within chased the cold away.

Polar bears were real enough but seldom seen as a kid, which made them more mythical and ghostly than anything else. Husky dogs were a more immediate problem. I was worried about polar bears, but I was scared to death of dogs. Well, not all dogs, I was always bringing a stray home. But other dogs—the ones that were chained, seemingly for life, and resented the fact you weren't—would willingly chew your arm off if extended in peace. I was terrified of them. And then there were the packs of half-starved dogs that roamed the edges of town finding strength in numbers. In the dead of winter, when hunger seized them, they would charge through the streets ripping and tearing at anything they could eat. They would gang up, injuring or killing the dogs on chains. A female dog in heat, tied up or not, was in for a heap of trouble. These were out-of-control Husky mongrels whose owners couldn't feed them. They were cut loose to fend for themselves and feral in every sense of the word.

Mom once bought me a pair of moosehide moccasins from the Dené people up on the hill. She tied them tightly to my heavily socked feet for a trip to the store. It was a crisp, bright morning when we set out, Mom holding my hand and the new moccasins sliding easily on the icy road. We hadn't made it far when I felt her grip tighten on my hand. Really tight. She stopped walking and pulled me towards her. Coming down the middle of the road in front of us was a pack of dogs. They were not snarly or menacing, some were wagging their tails, but they were bold. The dogs surrounded us, sniffing at my new moccasins. As they started fighting amongst themselves, Mom lifted me in her arms and turned for the house. The dogs began following and jumping up on her, trying to grab the moccasins and biting at my feet. It was now a race for home as they started to bite her in the back and legs. I was terrified. Mom dropped her mitts and with one hand undid the leather laces, pulled the moccasins off my feet, and threw them down on the ground for the dogs. We made it home. I remember Dad telling us to stay inside for the next few days. This happened more than a few times when I was growing up. We were told to stay inside until all the bad dogs were gone. We'd hear the shooting and see the dead dogs along the side of the road. It was always quiet after that.

A few years later, when I started school, we went through this dog cull again. It was the first time I recognized the word rabies in adult conversation. Anyone who had seen *Old Yeller* at the Igloo Theatre knew the meaning of that. From then on, whenever we saw a strange dog wandering the streets, we looked for the telltale sign of froth dripping from his mouth…yup, rabies.

There is a weight to long winter nights. Once the radio was turned off and the house went dark, I could feel it pressing me down into my bed and pushing away sleep. The banshee wind found new strength at night, carrying away any good thoughts I had as familiar trouble brewed in the back of my mind. I had no choice in what form The Bear visited my bedroom and invaded my dreams. He followed me throughout my childhood—a terrifying beast that came to life when I closed my eyes. Each night, dread flooded the room as my battle with The Bear began. It was unstoppable.

Come morning, and the promise of a new day, The Bear was all but forgotten. There were games to play, a quick breakfast to eat, and a tussle over the best set of mitts before heading out the door.

there is a weight to long winter nights.

"Bear on James Street last night, so you boys be careful," Mom warned my brother and me. Naturally, we took a side trip to look for bear tracks before heading over to Sonny's for road hockey. Day bears didn't matter as far as I was concerned. It was only the one that visited in the night that truly worried me.

Daylight was precious, what little of it there was, once winter came. Seemed you just got into whatever you were doing—building forts, endless games of road hockey, or leaping off rooftops into fresh snow—when it was dark again. There were no streetlights back then but luck would provide the moon on a rare night, and we would take advantage of it by staying out longer than we should have (excuses as to why firmly in place before heading home).

If the moon was out, it was a good bet the northern lights would be out too. While their grandeur was not entirely lost on us, they were mostly welcomed for the additional visibility they gave to whatever we were caught up in. Later in life, I would gaze up at the lights wondering how their beauty escaped me as a child and realize that wasn't the case. I do remember looking up in awe, an invisible hand with colored crayon scoring a luminous musical across the night sky. That was tempered when Big Hank, who was older than us, said if we looked at the lights without blinking for more than ten seconds, they would swoop down from the sky and snatch us up. I still catch myself counting.

It was one of those nights, clear and cold with the wind slackened off just enough. Bare bulbs aglow over porch doors, the moon, the stars, and a tinge of color in the northern sky were all we needed for a game of road hockey. No one remembered the score because we'd been playing for hours. It was late. My brother had left for home long ago, and I should have gone with him. I knew Mom would be mad, but I didn't care. We'd been cooped up in the house for days during the last storm. Storms always brought The Bear to wrestle sleep away—didn't they know that?

The game ended when Johnny Eleven decided he was done playing and wanted to go home. At least I could walk with him halfway. Things were OK until Johnny split off and disappeared into the dark. That's when I heard the dogs acting up. They usually howled a little at dusk before quieting down for the night, but they were really howling now. As fear percolated in the back of my mind, I began to run. The light in our kitchen came into view as I rounded the corner.

In the next instant, an implosion of dread and panic washed through my body, almost bringing me to my knees, as the reason for the dogs' dismay materialized before my eyes. A polar bear was on the road—the road I had to cross to get home. My short life was over.

Although my mind yielded itself to the fact I was a goner, the message never reached my legs. They recovered from the shock and a newfound force lifted me up over the road, passing so close in front of the bear that I thought I could touch him, and deposited me on the steps leading to the porch of my house.

Not quite sure what had happened, but flushed with joy and a love for all mankind, I dared to look back. The bear hadn't moved. His massive head, slung low to the ground, turned my way. For a dozen heartbeats our eyes locked, and then, with a faint huff, he turned away and started down the road. A wisp of frozen breath caught in the moonlight trailed behind him. I was pardoned by the bear's indifference.

Mom opened the porch door and, with a sternness that couldn't hide the worry, she asked, "Where were you?" I bravely ignored her question, pointed down the road, and said, "Bear on Herne Street."

There were more sinister works at play during the final years of my childhood. Far worse than anything the natural world could throw at me. It had such a grip on my mind that The Bear found itself playing second fiddle for a while.

Saturday matinees at the Igloo Theatre were the highlight of our week, and we usually left all fired up and ready to reenact the important scenes that involved swords, guns, or grenades. One Saturday the movie had none of that. It was about a submarine that broke down at sea, and when it finally got back to land everyone was dead. The Russians had dropped a nuclear bomb. No one felt like reenacting any part of that movie. What worried me was that I'd heard about nuclear bombs on the radio at home. Dad would hush us whenever talk of it came on. What was going on at the army base down the road? The Yanks had built an underground bunker at the end of the runway and a tower where soldiers with rifles stood on guard. Everything was top secret, but we could see the planes, big American bombers, flying around overhead day and night.

Why did we have to turn out all the lights and close the curtains when the siren went off? Where was Cuba and what were they doing with the Russians? Cold War? Well, it's cold here. Sheesh, they're going to drop a nuclear bomb on Churchill!

About thirty years ago, my friend Jack had a cabin and boat shed on the riverbank a few miles upstream from where the Churchill River empties into Hudson Bay. He spent a lot of time there fixing broken outboard motors or nailing yet another weathered plank onto to his shack, which was always under construction. His half-dozen Husky dogs sat chained in a line while he worked.

One afternoon towards the end of October, I drove across the tracks down along the shoreline where Jack was fiddling around his cabin putting stuff away for the winter. He was a childhood friend but not the easiest guy to get along with. You had to watch what you said or did around him. He was quick-tempered like his father and opinionated as hell, but still a good guy to visit if you caught him at the right time. He was in a good mood that day.

As we gossiped and laughed, I could see the river was making ice. All the creeks and streams upriver were freezing over, channeling fresh ice into the river's main body and carrying it downstream. At the same time, the river was flooding with tidal water from the bay. This ebb and flow of salt water in and fresh water out is a constant. It is the pulse of this hearty little community.

On a flood tide, salt water reaches over six miles (ten kilometers) up the river. In the fall, this causes the new freshwater ice that is pushing towards the mouth to stall, forming a sheet of ice than can span the river from bank to bank. The incoming tide had reached its highest point causing a huge ice jam in front of Jack's cabin.

The north wind numbed your face if you were oriented in that direction, so most of our visiting was done facing south. A good thing as that was the direction the huge polar bear was coming from. We could just make out the top of his back as he walked close to the river. He was downwind from the dogs so there was no alarm from them, but the bear had the wind and raised his massive head to sniff the air. He knew the smell of dogs. Some bears would turn away not wanting anything to do with them, but not this guy. There was always a chance of something to eat when there were dogs around.

Jack's dogs were a big problem for a polar bear—they would never give an inch to an oncoming bear when off their chains. They were big, burly Husky dogs bred for the harshest conditions with an ingrained hatred of the beast fast closing in on Jack and me. The bear was getting close when the dogs spotted him. They were enraged and lunged at the ends of their chains to get loose. Jack let two of his favorites off the line and the fight was on.

The bear was alarmed by the ferocity of the attack and turned towards the river, running flat out across the fresh ice, the dogs biting his rear every time they caught up. The old bear soon recovered from the sudden assault and slowed down as the battle moved out towards the middle of the frozen river. The dogs still lunged at the bear but lost some of their bravado as the old guy turned to face them lashing out with his huge paw in defense.

Traditionally, when Inuit hunters came across a polar bear on the ice, they would let loose their team of dogs. The dogs instinctively knew what to do and would surround and attack the bear from all sides. They would hold the bear at bay, wearing him down while he fought off the repeated attacks. When the hunter saw that the bear was growing tired, he would move in with his spear to finish him off. It was an important rite of passage for a young Inuit hunter.

Jack's two dogs would have had a hard time wearing this guy down. They were having enough trouble with the simple task of getting him to leave. From our point of view, it looked like a standoff out on the ice. The bear was sitting on his haunches and the dogs not fifty feet away. Neither the bear nor the dogs looked particularly tired. Every now and then, a dog would rush at the old bear, stop just short of his reach, and retreat back to where the other dog was sitting. The bear didn't seem to be worried about the dogs as there were not enough of them to do any harm. The dogs seemed to have lost heart but wouldn't take their eyes off of him for a second.

The tide that was holding the ice steady in one spot started to ebb. The huge span of ice was starting to break up and move towards the mouth

I grabbed this shot from a rigid inflatable boat. Bears always swim away from boats, making it tough to get a good shot. /A.B.

of the river. Jack saw what was coming and tried to call his dogs, but they were quite a ways out and either they couldn't hear him or were too occupied with the bear to acknowledge him. The strong current was churning the fractured ice into smaller bits that would be flushed into the bay. If the dogs couldn't be convinced to leave the bear and return home, all three would be going for the ride.

This was not a big problem for a polar bear, but it would probably be too much for the dogs. They faced being crushed by the fast-moving ice or drowning in the frigid water. Jack didn't want to lose his best dogs, so he grabbed his rifle, I grabbed my shotgun from the truck, and off we went to get their attention.

We worked our way closer as the ice shifted underneath our feet, but the dogs just wouldn't respond to his calls. Jack and I looked at each other and shook our heads in disbelief at our stupidity, but we were committed now and continued on. We never got the dogs' attention—it was the bear that found us interesting. The big brute got up, ignoring the lunges from the dogs, and started towards us. One hell of a situation we got ourselves into.

The bear continued to walk in our direction with the dogs coming along behind him. We turned and tried to scramble and scratch our way back to land. The ice was moving fast and we really had to watch our step. Falling in between fast-moving ice would have dire consequences, so we focused on the ice below and getting to shore as quickly as we could. The bear could have run us down in a heartbeat but stayed a measured distance behind. The dogs figured things out pretty quickly and ran past us towards the cabin. We were a few strides from shore when the bear closed the gap on us. Once our feet touched land, we had no choice but to turn and protect ourselves. Jack shot in front of the bear and it turned broadside, so I let loose with a No. 2 buckshot hitting him square in his big behind. Buckshot would do no lasting harm, not enough strength in the shot to break the skin, but I hoped it would send a clear message. He turned towards the moving ice and headlong into the first open patch of water he came to. Message received.

the business of bears

In the absence of any schooling beyond what some would consider the bare minimum, I missed the course in analytical thinking. I found it easy to let my mind wander, to take the easy way out, and not put too much pressure on myself with the clutter of facts and figures. I was good at it.

Polar bears were the perfect subject for me to lose myself in. I was born in their lap, stirred by their presence, and delighted in the thin air of excited fear that lingered in their wake. If ever there was a place to contemplate these fascinating creatures, it was Churchill, Manitoba.

When the business of polar bears began in the early 1980s, I was there to see it firsthand. All it took to kick-start the industry was a few well-known tour companies realizing that with just the right amount of discomfort to make it an adventure, you could bring people to see wild polar bears gathering and make a buck doing it. Throw in professional photographers and filmmakers who were always on the lookout for new opportunities and there you had it. They were all standing in line to get on that first buggy to Cape Churchill, thanks to my friends Dan and Len.

Len Smith is built low to the ground, barrel-chested with hands thick from gripping wrenches. A farm boy from the prairies who came north as a young man to ply his trade as a mechanic, he played hard and worked harder. When the work day was nearly over, he liked to gulp whiskey and cola from eight-ounce red plastic cups chilled with ice chipped from the windshield of his pickup truck.

Dan Guravich sipped scotch. Stately is the word that comes to mind when I think of him. Ramrod straight in stance and very much a gentleman—picture Mark Twain dressed for forty below—he was a biologist and photographer with a passion for polar bears. A man with a vision. Under any other circumstance there was no reason why these two men should have met. Given Dan's quest it was inevitable they would.

Cape Churchill juts into Hudson Bay like a hitchhiker's thumb. Follow the coast east from town for about thirty miles (fifty kilometers) and when it drops sharply to the south, there you are. In the late 1970s, Dan needed someone to help him get to there. Len was just the guy for the job.

In 1969, Dan got a taste of polar bears while working as the official photographer on the SS *Manhattan*, an ice-class oil tanker testing the frozen waters of the Northwest Passage looking for a viable route to ship crude. Seeing a polar bear in the wild is always an intense experience, but when Dan spotted his first one from the deck of the ship it was life changing. His concern for the well-being of these iconic animals grew and eventually led him to Churchill.

This scrappy little town was a trading post when Canada was in its infancy but the town endured. Like the tidal waters of Hudson Bay, the town's prospects ebb and flow but nothing is ever secure. Those that choose to live here also choose to accept hardship and isolation in exchange for freedoms only found on the frontier. When Dan first visited in the 1970s, we had no idea that our entire relationship with polar bears was about to be transformed. But Dan's vision and Len's hard work and tenacity brought to Churchill an era of change and hope, and a chance for a new identity, that would be recognized worldwide.

Len built big four-wheel drive buggies that could handle any terrain the rough country around Churchill had to offer. What Dan was looking for was something bigger, something that could take a small group of people, including himself, to Cape Churchill.

Cape Churchill was a place locals knew of but it had always remained a bit of a mystery, if only because it was near impossible to get to by land during the summer months and the rest of the year no one had any reason to go there. We knew the armed forces did cold weather training around the cape way back when. A few military observation towers still stood as a testament to those days. But Dan had heard, through his colleagues at Canadian Wildlife Service, that the cape was host to a large contingent of polar bears each fall. The gathering of bears at Cape Churchill would come to be called "a celebration." This was something he had to see.

Getting to the cape by land to witness the gathering was a logistical nightmare. Timing was critical. A small window of opportunity presented itself to anyone willing to trek over land and ice to get there. The challenge was given to Len. Could he build Dan a vehicle capable of carrying a group of adventurers to Cape Churchill, offering a place to eat and sleep protected from the elements and, most importantly, safe from polar bears?

Len is not the kind of guy who would say getting there is half the fun. For him, getting there is all the fun. He never tired of building something to get somewhere off the beaten path, be it an airboat to fly up the river during the spring high tide or an open deck four-wheel drive buggy to get his hunting buddies to where the birds were. He was a scrapyard innovator with a big hammer and twenty-ton jacks, but he was also a shrewd businessman. If he could get Dan to the cape, he knew nothing but good would follow.

Len framed up a metal box just over twenty feet (six meters) long, about eight feet (two and a half meters) wide, and seven feet (two meters) high. He wrapped it in white aluminum sheeting and fit drop-down windows from an old school bus along both sides. On the back, he put in a door and built a small deck. Inside, there were two rows of bus seats, five on the left and six on the right. Behind the row on the left, he put in an old, beat-up propane heater with a stack going through the roof directly overhead and a bit of shelving squaring off the sides and wall. Behind the seats on the right, he used spare pieces of plywood to box in a space from floor to ceiling with a bench across one side just big enough to sit on. He made a hole in the bench, placed a five-gallon bucket underneath, and screwed a toilet paper dispenser to the wall. After hanging a small mirror on the wall, the bathroom was complete.

He put the metal box atop an old, heavy frame resting on fat farm tractor tires and slid a gas engine underneath the floor with an extra-long stick shift leading up to the driver's seat. Two pieces of window glass angled across the front formed a windshield, complete with intermittent wipers. He added a door with a sliding window for the driver and on the back deck installed a steel ladder that tucked underneath, ready to drop down and welcome passengers aboard.

When Dan returned north the following fall, the first Tundra Buggy® was ready. After a successful trip to Cape Churchill to witness the polar bear celebration of 1980, Dan and Len wanted to make the experience available to others. In 1982, Len founded Tundra Buggy Tours and hired me as the first driver. From behind the wheel, I watched as the world was introduced to polar bears in the wild.

They were crazy times. No one knew for sure how this would play out—an eclectic mix of homemade buggies, decommissioned six-wheel drive army trucks, and half-track Bombardiers all crashing through the willows in hot pursuit of unsuspecting polar bears. We learned from our mistakes how not to be bullies and to do what the bears allowed us to do. Soon it became a challenge to find seats for everyone wanting to come to the show.

Next to watching polar bears, I like watching those who come to watch polar bears. The first sighting can be very powerful and more than a few are brought to tears. As a local, I sometimes overlook how far removed from the natural world people can be. Easy to forget I was raised closer to the ground than most.

One image etched in my mind took place on a tour years ago, as a handsome, middle-aged Asian woman stood alone on the back deck of one of the original buggied-up school buses. All the others had gone back inside, towards the front, to better view a few bears putting on a show. This woman chose to stay and was rewarded by a mature female polar bear that had appeared seemingly out of nowhere. The bear reared up and placed her large paws against the side of the deck, stretched her long, sinuous neck, and looked directly into the eyes of the startled but quickly composed woman. A few seconds passed between them. Then, with much grace, the woman put her palms together, held them close to her chin as in prayer, and bowed her head in reverence. It was a moment of intimacy that rattled me in a good way. It took a lady who had traveled halfway around the world to make me start seeing the bears in a different light.

I was too close-minded at the time to admit there could be any kind of a connection between man and wild beast, but I knew that something was going on. A few years and a few thousand hours of bear watching later, I found myself standing alone on the back deck of a newly built, much larger buggy enjoying a break from the group of photographers who were inside spooning hot chuck wagon soup. This was when Dancer first came to say hello.

A mother bear came along the ridge directly behind the buggy with two cubs trailing after her. She showed little interest in the huge machine, merely adjusting her path to the side to pass. Other than a sideways glance, she didn't care about me one bit. The first cub closed ranks and paid attention to its mother, but the second cub was out of sync and never fell into step. Instead, he came over to the side of the buggy and took a good long look at me. We had a bit of a conversation. Only when the photographers in the buggy caught on about the family group, thundering onto the back deck, did the little bear break away and trundle off towards his mother.

Over the next week or so, we began each day of the tour trying to find the mother and cubs. The family was not bothered by our presence as long as we were respectful. I got to know the little guy more and more everyday, talking to him and playing games. He would stand up to look for me over the edge of the deck if he heard my voice, dancing on his back legs. It was the start of a long friendship.

Over the next twenty years, we often found each other in early November just before the start of the hunt and visited until freeze-up. The bear of my childhood nightmares was replaced by a bear I could not wait to see.

I didn't think the new owners of Tundra Buggy Tours liked me much. Merv Gunter and his wife were a poster couple for clean living. I could have been the poster boy for a Grateful Dead concert. I first met him when he was the local bank manager. Later, he and his wife started a small tour company for viewing polar bears in Churchill. When they bought Tundra Buggy Tours in 1999, they took over the largest tour company in town. Under any other circumstances, they would have had nothing to do with me. But I had a few things to offer. One they needed and one they would want.

When Len handed over Tundra Buggy Tours to the Gunters, they found themselves in a situation where most of the corporate knowledge was not there. Since I'd been part of the whole business of polar bear viewing since the beginning, I had experience dealing with both the machinery and the bears. The company needed frontline guys, like me, who'd spent the last twenty years or so working with Len. There were a few who could help, but most were employed full-time elsewhere and couldn't be there on a regular basis. I could. I also had an idea that I hoped would get me back out on the tundra, the place I needed to be, because I was addicted to polar bears.

I was a bumbling idiot when it came to computers and the Internet, but one night I landed on a website with video of wild animals at a watering hole in South Africa. I was mesmerized. It was a live feed from Kruger National Park by a site called Africam.com. These guys pioneered the use of real-time video in exotic places filming wild animals. My mind was spinning at the possibilities as I watched a pride of lions, elephants, and hyenas all captured by the camera. If only I could do this with polar bears here at home.

Without thinking anything through, I immediately sent Africam.com a message asking if they would be interested in doing what they do only half a world away with polar bears. I resigned myself to the fact I would be completely ignored. Never expected a reply. But I opened my e-mail in the morning and read, "Yes, we are interested in polar bears. How do we do it?" It was a good question.

The options were limited as to how I could pull it off. In reality, there was only one. I had to convince Merv that we should go into partnership broadcasting polar bears to the world live via the Internet and maybe make a few bucks doing it. Tundra Buggy Tours held the majority of permits needed to operate individual commercial vehicles in the Churchill Wildlife Management Area, and in order for me to have a fighting chance at this I needed the use of one of those permits.

Sitting in Merv's office set me on edge. The last time I faced him across a desk he refused me a loan. This time I had his interest. He was a man who sat with confidence in his chair. Although he tried to keep a poker face, I could see he was intrigued by my proposal. He knew I had a great idea in the live polar bear feed, potentially the first of its kind to be broadcast on the World Wide Web or anywhere on the planet. We both knew that all of the permits he held were seldom used at one time. There was a way to fit me in without losing money if one permit was tied up with me and the camera. He saw the potential, and possible benefits, with little capital investment. He wasn't such a bad guy. Unexpectedly, he was giving me a shot. I was more than grateful.

Still he was understandably leery. I did have a reputation as something of a pirate, but he needed someone like me around to help him avoid costly mistakes with equipment and lives. He needed someone who knew bears, buggies, and the difficult terrain they both travel. He could put up with my less than desirable appearance—long hair, graying beard, and a love of good Canadian whiskey—if I could avert some of the inevitable screwups any new owner was going to make. A polar cam would put me out there on the ice with his other buggies. This was a partnership that could benefit both of us.

Old Buggy One, the original buggy Len built, was given to me for the Polar Bear Cam. It had been decommissioned and forgotten, broken and rusting in the boneyard. A resurrection was needed. It soon became painfully clear that I was the one to do it with little or no help from the guys in the shop. They were overloaded trying to keep up with repairs and maintenance of the fleet of buggies soon to go online for the upcoming bear season. It would be no easy task getting Buggy One into a state where I could drive it—and live in it—for the seven or eight weeks I needed to broadcast. But it had to be done if I wanted to get back to where the bears were. The shop guys were great and helped when they could. With inspirational bouts of cussing and well-managed beer breaks, somehow it all came together. I just had to wait for the guys from South Africa to show up with the camera.

Until the three of them walked through the door of the airport terminal in Churchill, the whole thing seemed a bit over the top. A guy like me shouldn't have been able to pull it off, but there they were, as excited and pumped as I was to get this thing up and running. Damn, it was a good feeling.

The amount of gear the guys brought was staggering. For someone whose head developed a dull throb at the mere thought of sitting in front of a computer, it was overwhelming and it reinforced the fact that I knew little about the technology behind what we were trying to do. "He's a bear guy, not a computer guy" is how Paul from Africam.com explained my limited grasp of how things worked to his team back in Johannesburg.

All of this happened in 1999, when computers were still big and clunky and beeped and blinked and whirred. The beat-up, old buggy hosting a state-of-the-art Internet broadcast studio was in itself contradictory, but so much so that it all made sense.

At this point, a person well-versed in all the applications that were needed to get the live-feed out would fill you with techno talk. Fifteen years ago, most of you would have been left wondering what he was talking about. Today, I am sure, it's only a small section of people who wouldn't understand. The buggy set-up itself was simple, really. There was a camera mounted on the roof that was operated from inside with a satellite dish to upload the live feed. The camera was a pan-tilt-zoom with side-mounted infrared lights for night filming. In its simplicity, it would open up a window into the life of polar bears to anyone with access to the World Wide Web.

Buggy One, now given a second life, was parked and waiting at the Tundra Buggy Lodge along the coast of Hudson Bay, about nineteen miles (thirty kilometers) east of Churchill. The setting was perfect. The Hudson Bay Lowlands are a landscape of low-lying willow and scrub brush. Wrinkles of sand and cobble beach ridges radiate back from the bay's high tide mark. With little ground relief, on a clear day you can look across a small tidal pool towards the morning sun and spot a polar bear coming over the horizon. This is the direction in which they come when the migration starts. The same direction Buggy One's big front window was facing.

The days spent with the guys from South Africa setting up the camera and the lead-up to the broadcast were heady, even without the libations. Anticipation of the event manifested itself in uncontrollable smiles on all of our faces, while good Canadian whiskey eased the anxiety. There was a lot riding on this for me and everyone else involved. Long hours, worry and sweat, loads of money tied up in equipment and travel, and the investment by Tundra Buggy Tours all reinforced the need for this to be successful. The equipment was ready. We were ready. We just needed a polar bear.

Buggy One still plays host to the Polar Bear Cam

Working with the world's finest wildlife filmmakers and photographers, I've learned that storytelling is everything and that everything in the wild has a story to tell. The tale I wanted to tell with the Polar Bear Cam was one that has entertained and fascinated me for years; a visual story that unfolds before your eyes, as thrilling and dramatic as any well-written screenplay. With a constant change of settings and light and characters, there is no shortage of drama out on the tundra.

The scene is set in late fall with a land barren to the untrained eye. The landscape is filled with deep reds and darkening shades of brown against the ever-changing blue of the bay. Vegetation along the coast is spent, drawing in to fortify itself for the long, cold months ahead. Strokes of lime grass, tall in the face of the wind, follow the ancient beach ridges. Clouds hurry across the sky chased by a gathering north wind. No snow yet.

Inside Buggy One, the story begins at an exciting pace with camera ready and waiting for the first wave of bears from the east. There is elation and relief when they are first spotted coming this way. Over the next few days, more bears show up. Some are leery and give the buggy a wide berth when passing but others waltz right by. I seek out old friends and am thrilled when I find them. Time has taught me that each bear is an individual with unique mannerisms and behavior that is revealed if you look for it. I quickly see if the past year has been a rough one if their weight is down, if they want to be left alone to rest, or if they are energized and looking to mix it up with a willing partner—all true indicators of a bear's well-being. Very quickly the scene shifts. It gets colder, the ponds freeze over, and the bears are delighted with new ice underfoot. They meet in the middle to socialize. And day by day, they keep arriving.

With the first dusting of snow the land changes dramatically. A clean, white slate presents itself but, as more bears arrive, fresh tracks in the snow add a new dimension. Ice starts to build along the bay's edge reaching further out each day. The bears take notice and become more animated. As their activity level picks up, the sparring is more spontaneous and doesn't seem to stop.

Mothers and cubs start to arrive next. It's a good day when you see one healthy cub, but two cubs gives you hope. A mother with three cubs is not unheard of and, if you get a chance to see this, you can't help but be in awe of the courage and strength the mother has to keep her offspring together and alive through such unimaginable hardships. It truly is a testament to the extraordinary will and survival skills these bears have. Not all family groups fare as well. New, inexperienced mothers or ones that are sick can have a hard time of it. It is gut-wrenching to see a mother unable to feed her cubs because, for whatever reason, her milk is gone. There is despair and panic in her eyes and you know this family will suffer the greatest losses.

Bears continue to make their way towards the coast from all directions as sub-zero temperatures set in. Day and night, there is activity everywhere you look. Bad young bears, smart old bears, and everything in between, are meeting each other, running away from each other, wrestling, digging, rolling, and sleeping. Mothers and cubs dodge big males or turn to challenge them face to face. The new ice on the bay is now being tested by the anxious and hungry. The drama builds as the bears start looking to the north, older ones reaching for smells high in the air coming off the new ice, offering a hint it will soon be time to go.

Then Old Man Winter says "enough is enough" and slams his icy fist on the ground. The storm is blinding and shakes you to the bone. The north wind threatens to lift the buggy and send it tumbling into the abyss. It goes on far too long. You catch yourself worrying for your safety. Then all is calm. The storm has past. Hudson Bay is covered with ice as far as the eye can see and not one polar bear is in sight.

This story, like your favorite Christmas movie, is repeated every year. There are bit players, like the Arctic fox, Willow and Rock Ptarmigans, Snowy Owl, and the regal Ivory Gull. An ever-changing sky and the long, dark night that bursts into color with the cueing of the aurora borealis have reoccuring roles as well. This was the story I wanted to tell, and I believed the Polar Bear Cam would make it possible.

The Polar Bear Cam made history one day in early October 1999. It was unfortunate the South African boys weren't there to witness it in the raw. They had to fly out the day before and were resting in a hotel in New York City. I got ahold of them on the phone when the first polar bear came into view on the monitor. It was an unforgettable moment and the

The Tundra Buggy Lodge at Polar Bear Point in October

start of what I thought would be a new, fulfilling chapter in my life. One that would bring me, and as many people I could reach, countless hours of pleasure and an understanding of these sometimes maligned and misunderstood but always amazing animals.

People loved the Polar Bear Cam. The first season was a huge success and had everyone buzzing. It became the most watched critter cam on the web. At the end of the season, I was thrilled by what we'd accomplished and completely exhausted. By the time winter set in and the last bear was out on the ice, I had spent seven weeks in Buggy One operating the camera from the coast of Hudson Bay. The night vision footage was proof that the action never stopped. A big, old bear emerging from the dark into the infrared lights was as dramatic as it could get. I wanted to give the audience as much as possible and thought the night shoots enhanced the overall experience for the viewer, so I grabbed a few hours of rest whenever I could, but I was sleep deprived for much of the time. I was having such a good time, I didn't care.

Taking over the business was a huge learning curve for Merv and, I'm sure, a difficult one. While Len was an outstanding mechanic and inventor who was completely at home with a wrench in his hand, Merv had spent the last twenty years behind a banker's desk. Maintaining the equipment was a huge part of the business and required a skilled manager who could keep everything running.

One of the reasons I ran the bear cam near Gordon Point most of the time was that it made me available to help with the operations onsite and lend my experience when needed. My contribution to the company was to be there not if, but when problems arose. There was not a hope in hell of me filling Len's shoes, but after twenty years in the industry, I could help to troubleshoot the inevitable issues that came with working in such harsh conditions.

The whole business of polar bear viewing began with that first buggy trip to Cape Churchill in the fall of 1979. It evolved to include day tours out of Churchill to the Gordon Point area roughly fifteen miles (twenty-four kilometers) along the coast east of Churchill. Each year, the cape trip was scheduled to make a move from Gordon Point on November the seventh. It consisted of two nine-day tours and was a must for serious photographers, filmmakers, and the well-traveled. It was the trip of a lifetime to a place unmatched for polar bear viewing. World famous, and deservedly so, Cape Churchill was magical. I had to get out there with the Polar Bear Cam, one way or another.

In the early days, getting to Cape Churchill could be troublesome but barring any mechanical failure was usually done in a day. We'd leave at first light and arrive by dusk. Heavy snow fall was the biggest headache for the trip as far as natural obstacles were concerned. A slight change in temperature in the late 1980s screwed everything up. What was once a sure thing—the ground, lakes, and creeks freezing over and enabling the buggies to travel over land for the first half of the trip—was no longer a certainty. Machinery was breaking through the ice cover on the lakes, and streams were running wide open. The La Pérouse Bay delta, where buggies must traverse over ice from tundra to the frozen edge of Hudson Bay in the final leg of the journey, was now treacherous and unpredictable. The ice covering the delta was becoming thinner each November.

In the coming years, it was hit or miss to make it to the cape in a day. Making it to the cape for the first tour rarely happened. The ground just wasn't freezing in time. At the time the company changed owners, there had only been one year in the past seven that both of the Cape Churchill trips were without setbacks or delays.

This was the scenario faced by Merv his third winter, the first year Len was completely out of the picture. The year before, the buggy train never made it and both tours spent their time at La Pérouse Bay, halfway to Cape Churchill. The overland route was proving to be a disaster and now impossible to use.

Buggy One, which became a place for the staff and drivers to relax after the day on the tundra, was parked at the end of the lodge just past the kitchen and utility trailer of the buggy camp. A buggy camp, or buggy train, is essentially a series of train cars—sleeper, dining, and lounge—but the steel wheels have been swapped with large rubber tires. It was mid-November and the season's first Cape Churchill tour was still at the lodge site east of Gordon Point. The overland route was impassable but the cape trip was crucial. The bears that gathered at Gordon Point left for the hunt earlier than the group gathered at Cape Churchill because that stretch of Hudson Bay freezes before the waters swirling around the cape. The polar bears around the lodge had all gone, a few stragglers could be seen hurrying onto the ice, and every one of the drivers and staff knew it was over. If they didn't get to the cape for the second tour, there would be nine days without anything to show the guests and it would be devastating.

The buggy camp drivers and lodge staff had a meeting in Buggy One. I was not part of the meeting, since I wasn't an employee of Tundra Buggy Tours, but I listened to what was being discussed. There was consensus amongst them that they, as a group, would ask Merv to cancel the second cape trip. The timing was critical as guests were now on the verge of making their way to Churchill for the tour. If the trip was going to be canceled, it had to be done now. Back in Churchill, it sounded like Merv was contemplating the idea as well. To cancel thirty-six bookings for the most expensive and prestigious trip of the season was a huge decision and, given the track record of past troubles of getting to the cape, it could very well prove disastrous to the financial stability of the company. Cape Churchill bookings would drop right off if clients considered it a gamble that they would actually get there. Hell, how was I going to get the camera to the cape if it all fell apart before my eyes?

Len worked hard to build the business to what it was when he sold it. He accomplished this because he was tenacious, he was driven, and he was as stubborn as a mule. A few times when we were fighting our way to the cape, I'd mentioned a route that might be better than what we were up against now. Not a hope in hell he would consider it. He thought the hardships faced getting to the cape were part of the overall experience. Most of us who did the grunt work didn't think so, but he was the boss.

Now was the time to try the new route. I just had to intercept Merv when he arrived at camp before the gang got to him. News came before he arrived that he had made up his mind to cancel and was coming to meet everyone and give them his decision in person. Crap!

I grabbed him when he arrived at camp that night. I was blunt. I told him that if he gave me a buggy the next morning, I would have a new route before noon. He decided he had nothing to lose and agreed. The crew was visibly upset when he told them I was going to try a new route. Their minds were made up to go home. Now I had to deliver.

I left early the next morning with two other employees. Instead of going inland, I hung close to the edge of the bay on the landfast salt water ice that had recently formed along the coast. It was like a super highway and we made it to the cape in two and a half hours—the fastest trip ever. The next morning they broke camp, hauled everything to Cape Churchill, and were set up within seven hours. Merv owed me one.

...we had no idea that our entire relationship with polar bears was about to be transformed.

D.C.

I love these old bears.
All banged up from a
lifetime of struggle.
They live mostly on wits
and lessons learned,
each face with a thousand stories.

D.C.

waiting for dancer

My first cup of coffee warmed my chilled hands. It was the second year of the six I would operate the Polar Bear Cam from Buggy One. Through the window, I watched the November sun as it broke the horizon, flooding the eastern sky with promise. That's when I felt the bump. There was a bear banging on the side of my buggy demanding my attention. By the force he used, I could tell without looking that he was a big boy. With caution I leaned over the driver's seat and scraped away a small patch of frost from the side window.

A full-grown polar bear standing on his hind legs could easily punch out the glass, so I was reluctant to present my mug as a target until I could figure out the temperament of my early morning visitor. From a few feet back, all I could see was a wide black nose pressed against the sliding window at the bottom of the door frame—a full eight feet from the ground. The bear was drawing in smells through the window, processing all the information that was important to him through his nose. As I scraped away some more ice, the bear pulled his massive head back and looked me square in the eyes. Damn, he was big…and familiar. I knew this bear.

After years of working in close proximity to polar bears you pick up on signs that let you know the disposition and character of the animal. For me, the eyes were the most important tell, a bear's resume if you will. There was no fear or anger in the eyes of the bear looking back at me nor was there alarm. What I saw was an expression that said, "Hey! Remember me?" If the big brute had had a tail longer than a few inches, I'm sure it would have been wagging.

It was Dancer! How did he find me? I was completely shocked. And entirely thrilled. I hadn't seen him in ages. He was always a Cape Churchill bear, and I'd stopped making that trek years before.

Little did I know that this would be the rekindling of an improbable relationship, suspicious to a few and fascinating to many, but one that would bring me countless hours of pure joy and a smattering of conflict. For a few weeks every November for the next five years, Dancer would keep me company. He staked out his territory under the driver's door window and never gave an inch to any bear brave or silly enough to cross the invisible line drawn in the snow.

As far as polar bears go, Dancer was a near perfect specimen. He was a lump of a bear with well-defined muscle even below a thick layer of fat. I'm sure his ponderous behind, the true measure of a polar bear's health and stature, was eyed with envy and caution by other males and, no doubt, convinced more than a few ladies that he was the one. If a polar bear's hunting prowess is directly related to the size of his rear end, then Dancer took a back seat to no other. I would say he was around twelve years old when he made the trek from the cape to visit for the first time. The scars on his broad face from battling over the ladies or protecting a kill told me he was a warrior approaching his prime. The respect shown by other bears was evident, and the few challenges to his authority were quickly dealt with.

The usual procedure when one male bear approaches another is a type of slow tango where both animals delicately circle one another, heads slung low to the ground, eye contact never broken, making sure all of their assets are on full display. The dance varies in length, as an observer it seems to go on and on, but it ends when one bear decides his assets don't match up and trundles off. Size is a factor but it is not uncommon to see a large bear give ground to another of lesser stature. I believe it has to do with the degree of intimidation seen in the eyes. Dancer wouldn't tango. He had his own way of dealing with intruders. The first time I saw him in action, I went from shock to amazement to spasms of laughter within seconds.

The window Dancer used when he would visit slid open wide enough that when standing on his back legs he could shove his head through to his ears. We were having one of our early morning get-togethers over a cup of coffee, one of his favorite smells, when I noticed a big male bear making his way toward us. The bear's slow plodding brought him quite close before he stopped to collect his thoughts. He was figuring out if it was in his best interest to check out what was going on or to use prudence and alter his course. He chose to continue our way.

Once his mind was made up, the newcomer's approach changed. Like a ship beating into the wind, he started tacking, changing course every so often, angling his way closer, and giving careful thought to every step. His progress was slowed even further by long pauses to watch for any reaction from Dancer. By now, any other bear would have taken notice and either hightailed it out of there or turned to meet the challenge head on. Not Dancer. He knew the bear was there but ignored him completely. It got to the point where I wondered if I should break our visit short and close the window, so Dancer wouldn't be caught off guard. At that moment, my friend let out a big snort that dampened the air inside the buggy and pushed himself away from the window to sort things out.

Like a reluctant ballerina, Dancer balanced himself on one leg and did a wobbly pirouette to face his adversary. The momentum of such a maneuver caused him to plop down on his greatest asset with such force I'm sure I felt the buggy shake. There he sat, looking like a fuzzy white Buddha, waiting to dish out a bit of enlightenment to the bear frozen in midstride not forty feet away.

The next move was left entirely up to the uninvited visitor, who I could see was giving great thought as to how he should handle this unexpected and tenuous situation. The choice to back away should have been given more consideration. The bear gave a great yawn and, ever so slowly, lowered his front paw to take his last step forward.

Dancer drew his head in close to his massive shoulders and flew at the unfortunate beast, ramming him with such force that it lifted him off his feet and sent him tumbling through the air in a slow arc and landing in a confused heap. In a heartbeat, he was upright and running flat out for his life.

No, Dancer was no ordinary bear.

The first time I found myself within yards of a huge male polar bear reared up on his hind legs to duke it out with another, I was in awe. The power and intensity of what was taking place before me was completely mesmerizing. When the sparring started, I maneuvered the camera buggy close to the action. I swear the buggy shook whenever they collided.

Dancer was one half of the duo going toe-to-toe. When another bear approached and the two hit it off, Dancer would lead the way to the cushy kelp beds or to the willow breaks where snow had drifted on the lee side. As tough as these bears are, there will be no roughhousing without something soft for them to land on.

I was right in the thick of it, watching the small flurries of snow they kicked up burst with sparkle when caught by the light. This was the first time I was this close, alone without any distractions, so close that everything around me disappeared—all of my senses were in play and piqued. I could hear the muddled thud as one bear stood and delivered a blow with both paws to the chest of the other, trying to knock him off his back legs, and the deep grunts and faint squeals as one was forced to the ground reluctantly surrendering. Muscles and fat rippled under their great white coats while frozen packets of breath suspended over their heads momentarily before drifting up and away. It's a spectacle not easily matched in nature. You could easily forget it was all play and done out of pure joy.

The experts will tell you this sparring is just practice for the real thing when the big males fight it out on the spring ice for the nod of a fine maiden. Any researcher, scientist, or rose-cheeked tour guide will tell you there is well-defined reasoning behind this activity: it builds strength and stamina for the rigors that lay ahead. I've seen tourists left a bit puzzled, wondering if they should be trying to ask pertinent scientific questions when, in fact, they really just want to watch the bears. Which is exactly what I think they should do. I tell them to enjoy the moment, the bears certainly are.

Dancer loved to wrestle. When he found a suitable partner who matched him in strength and temperament it could be hours, and sometimes days, of rolling and tumbling and biting and boxing. After sliding belly first into a bank of snow to cool down, and taking a short rest, they would be up and at it again. There was no clear winner when they would spar, each had equal time being thumped to the ground. It was not a contest in which anyone wanted to dominate, that would be no fun. On a rare occasion there would be specks of blood on the fur and rarer still if one of the combatants got mad. It wasn't unusual to catch sight of the bears grappling right through the night. Their energy seemed boundless.

All of this flies in the face of those "in the know." If you were to listen to the experts, or read any number of papers put out by researchers, they would describe these bears during the time spent off the ice as in a state of walking hibernation. The bears would be called sluggish, lethargic, or in energy conservation mode. This may be true during long summer days when temperatures can reach 80° F (27° C) and cause overheating. With the weight of their great coats and heavy with fat, the bears would not want to do much of anything. Come fall, when weather cools and the bears have shed a lot of their weight, their energy levels go through the roof. I can't help but scratch my head when those "in the know" point to a polar bear and say that it is conserving energy and that's why it appears slow and plodding. And then the bear slowly plods over to bite another bear on the behind, signaling the start of a round of intense sparring that will last the rest of the day. This behavior does not comply with what the experts tell us.

The majority of bears, after a long summer and fall on land, are not near starvation, suffering from any malaise, or existing in some kind of zombie state. They are healthy and content and looking for someone to wrestle with. When the winter is almost here, and soon there will be seals to hunt, they can feel it. Time to mix it up a bit.

Not all the bears like to spar of course. The old timers are usually too cranky, others are hungry, tired, or hurt, and some are just plain shy and have not figured out how to socialize. At this time of the year, most mother bears are exhausted, continually on guard against the threat of other bears harming their cubs, so it is heartwarming to see a healthy family that has found respite from worry and watch as they enjoy a lively round of push and shove.

This type of social behavior was not evident in the early 1980s, but I watched as it evolved right before my eyes. When I first started coming to this stretch of coastline near Gordon Point there was no sparring. I'd never heard of sparring. The bears, for the most part, kept to themselves. It was exciting when two bears approached one another—the best we hoped for was a bit of shoving or a short game of tag. I can only offer speculation as to why the bears began this behavior in earnest thirty years ago.

When this whole business of bears started there was a small, eclectic mix of machinery and people who would bounce their way out here from town for the day looking for bears. They found them scattered along the coast and back in the willow breaks. There was no concentration of polar bears. Not like today. In the mid-1980s, the only bears you really saw gathered together were families with young cubs. Occasionally, you would find two or three bears within eyesight of each other or a pair of older siblings laying together and that was a rare and exciting find. Almost all of the bears were wary and skittish when the vehicles arrived and reacted to any unnatural noise with concern, like the opening of a metal-framed buggy, the rev of an engine, or loud people. Some bears hightailed it into the tall willows never to be seen again. In the beginning, the rule was to spot the bear and shut down whatever you were riding in, remain quiet, and wait for the bear to get over its nervousness. Innate curiosity would overrule caution, in most cases, and eventually a polar bear would make its way towards the vehicle. The ones that did come over never really let their guard down and bolted at any disturbance.

After a few seasons, the bears that returned to this area each fall became a bit more relaxed around the machines. The sounds became familiar and they knew there was no threat. A parked vehicle would attract a bear, and then another would come along and then another. Their need to know what was going on brought them together.

As the business of bears grew, there was more demand for access to this area, which meant more vehicles and new ideas to expand the industry. Camping out with the bears was one idea that caught on. Expeditions to Cape Churchill had been going on for a few years using a homemade mobile buggy camp to travel and live in, and the same camp was now set up closer to Churchill in the Gordon Point area, where day-trippers from town were offered the option of "living" with the bears for five days. Meals had to be prepared for the campers and, as you can imagine, a hungry polar bear found the smells to be irresistible.

A combination of cooking and curiosity brought bears from miles away to the area, particularly to the buggy camp. There was a hierarchy: the tough warriors ruled the area immediately surrounding the camp with lesser bears hanging around the peripheral and family groups skirting the far edges. It was during this time that the bears found themselves sharing an area much smaller than they were used to. They were suddenly so close to each other that interaction could not be helped. With only a faint promise of something to eat and some distractions from the camp and day-trippers, the bears turned to one another to occupy their time. If they left the area they might miss out on something, so the bears stayed close and kept an eye open for any opportunity. As a result they got to know one another in a setting that was anything but threatening. Why not wrestle?

You will find no mother on the planet that will protect and nurture her offspring to the degree a polar bear will.

—D.C.

an education

Something was up. From inside Buggy One I watched as a slightly underweight cub, acting a bit strange, tried to walk in the deep tracks left in the snow by my pal Dancer. The footprints were the size of a catcher's mitt, easy to step into, but it was the distance in between them that was the problem. It was a big stretch for the little guy to hit every hole, yet it didn't stop him from trying. I consider myself pretty familiar with the locals, and I hadn't noticed the cub until Dancer showed up for his annual visit. He must have been following him for some time. I had to keep my eye on this one.

The next morning, Dancer was lying at his usual spot just below the driver's door window and watching from the edge of the willows was the little bear. The cub had an all-encompassing interest in the big bear and wouldn't take his eyes off him. Over the next few days, Dancer played like the little guy didn't exist as he followed his every move.

After spring romance out on the ice, male bears like Dancer move on without a worry about the outcome or parenting duties to attend to. Yet I wondered if there was a connection between them. Could this be one of Dancer's cubs? It was not an impossible stretch to think so. He knew the cub was tagging along behind him, no way he could not, but he didn't seem to mind.

Science says that the big males, when given the opportunity, will kill young bears. I have witnessed it on a few occasions—it's not a pretty sight—but don't believe this behavior is true of all bears. And I would like to think it's not true of Dancer. I've spent a great deal of time observing bears in the fall, when most are at their hungriest. In my experience, it is rare to see an adult bear make a determined effort to take a cub. In fact, most of the big males are indifferent to the young.

So, what was going on between the cub and Dancer? It soon became clear: this was how the little bear was surviving. At a safe and respectful distance, the little bear was continuing his education. He was acquiring the skills needed to become a successful hunter and picked one of the best to learn from. Dancer was in his prime and a true warrior. He had a lot to offer both in lessons and in leftovers. When a seal kill is made, big males strip and eat only the fat off their prey, leaving plenty for a young bear to feed off.

It's incredible how quickly these young bears have to adapt to survive. They have to use their intelligence and instinct each minute of the day to get by. What an incredibly worrisome time it must be for the cub that has just been driven out by its mother.

The little bear was going on his third year, probably chased away by his mother during spring courtship. Although there were many lessons learned from her, he still had a long and hard road to go to ensure survival. When he adopted Dancer, he started on the right path.

One of the most haunting experiences I have encountered in my years of bear viewing took place during a blinding snowstorm along the coast of Hudson Bay. The ice had set and the bears were leaving for the winter hunt. The relentless wind roared, driving the wet snow on a long angle into the ground. I couldn't move the buggy, and I wouldn't dare until I could see where I was going. Drifting in and out of the wail I heard a sharp cry not unlike that of a newborn baby. It was hard to determine which way it was coming from. The windows were icing over and the chance of seeing what was making the disturbing sound was slim, but I knew what it was. The wind fell back for half a second and the polar bear cub came into view, disappearing back into the storm just as quickly.

There are more than a few reasons for a young bear to be alone and afraid. Regardless of how this came to be, it was heartbreaking. It does not matter how hardened you are, the sight of that lost little bear frantic with fear and worry would have brought a lump to your throat. If you are in touch with your humanity, when a young one is in trouble you share its pain. No matter the species. I felt helpless when I saw the cub but took comfort in knowing that the mother would not stop looking for the young one if they were separated.

You will find no mother on the planet that will protect and nurture her offspring to the degree a polar bear will. The hardships she must suffer during the first year of their lives are extraordinarily severe. She has so much of herself invested in their survival that the term "abandoned" does not apply. There are no abandoned polar bear cubs. Separated or orphaned? Yes. Others may be pushed away by the mother because she is mating or pregnant, which usually happens when it is time for the cubs to go on their own at the age of two or three. But a mother unwillingly separated from her cubs will never stop searching for them.

Young cubs found alone are rare, whatever the circumstances, and have a real fight on their hands to survive. However, one cannot discount instinct at any age. Other family groups might accept an orphaned cub, but for most cubs orphaned before their first season on the ice the outlook is not good. It's a cruel fate but one that is part of the cycle of nature—and one that we have no business sticking our nose in.

If polar bear cubs survive their first year, they are well on their way. They learn invaluable lessons from their mothers during the four months of winter and spring spent hunting seal out on the ice and into the summer months on land. Who are we to say they are not capable of surviving on their own come fall? It would be hard but not impossible. Polar bears are so remarkable because their survival instincts are constantly evolving. If only a small percentage of orphaned cubs survive, then it makes the species that much stronger, that much more capable of overcoming whatever Mother Nature has in store for them.

I felt good about the little guy that was tailing Dancer. He had a fighting chance at making it. Watching the way the cub mimicked him was fascinating. When the big bear went on a walkabout, the cub would not let him get far before he started off behind him. Dancer would make frequent stops, planting his fist-sized nose flat on the ground and breathing in large volumes of information to sort out. When the cub came upon the same spots, he would put his nose flat to the ground like Dancer had. When Dancer rolled on the ice to clean his great coat, the little guy did the same. This is typically how any cub would learn, but he was doing it at a distance without the close comfort and protection only a mother could provide.

One bit of behavior left me tickled. Bears can flop down almost anywhere for a short nap, but when they feel a big snore coming on they need to dig a day bed. They go to great lengths to find the perfect location with the ideal texture of snow. Bears can be quite fussy in the construction of these beds and Dancer was no exception. When it was time for the big sleep, I watched as the big bear finally found a suitable spot heavy with snow and began the exacting task of removing just the right amount. Using his massive paws as an excavator, he carved and pushed and shoveled until he felt he had it right. He tried it out for size and comfort only to get up carve and push a little more. Like a dog, he followed his stub of a tail around in a circle within the bed before flopping down for the start of a long, deep slumber only to discover it still was not right. He got up, found another spot, and started over. After the new bed was finally made, and the big bear satisfied and settled, the ever-attentive cub seized the moment and crawled into the abandoned bed to enjoy a comfortable sleep alongside his benefactor. For the little bear, everything was perfect.

Mid-September at Gordon Point can be a volatile time with easterly winds that bring nothing but crap weather for days on end. Sleet and driving rain are not uncommon, but on this day there was bright sunshine, not a breath of wind, and just a hint of fall in the air. A full tide and a lazy sea made it all quite serene.

I knew there was a big old bear somewhere close by, and my intent was to film him lolling around, I hoped, in a swath of colourful fireweed or some situation with contrasting vegetation. Instead I found a mother bear with a yearling bumping along behind, walking along the ancient beach ridge that points out onto the bay. When they got to the end, she and the cub slipped into the water with barely a ripple. The cub quickly took his place just over her shoulder, so he could swim when possible and grab onto her when tired.

You can watch bears swim for a long ways if the bay waters are calm, but if there is any sea at all they disappear amongst the swell and chop. That day the sea was still. The pair swam straight out from land until lost in the valleys of the long swell. There was nothing out there. In the direction the bears were going they could swim for hundreds of miles and not reach land. I couldn't figure it out.

I continued on my way, driving along the shoreline and hoping to run into something interesting, often looking back and out to sea with the binoculars for any sign of their return. The day was wearing on, so I doubled back following the same route I came. I stopped when a flash of white at the edge of the tideline caught my attention. With the binoculars, I saw the mother emerge from the water, the cub close behind, with a freshly killed seal in her mouth. Quite a sight. While enjoying my good fortune, it struck me that there was not a bit of ice as far as the eye could see and wouldn't be for another month or so. Without the platform of ice to hunt for seal the polar bear is unable to sustain itself, or so the experts would lead us to believe, but right in front of me was a mother enjoying a meal with her cub. And I think I know how she did it.

It is surprising how close you can get to a seal when he is having a snooze. On a warm sunny day with a calm sea, no doubt the chance of finding a sleeping seal is pretty good—they rest while floating on top of the water. A mother with a cub in tow must have exceptional hunting skills to pull this off, and there might be another reason she ended up with the seal, but watching her swim away I sensed she knew what she was doing.

There is a lot of controversy about the fate of this population of polar bears. With the wonky weather and the bombast from conservation organizations preaching certain doom, it all becomes a bit messy. The experts who make up the advisory boards of these organizations, the ones most quoted in the press, will not admit or at least give a nod to the fact that these bears are adapting to the challenges Mother Nature has been throwing at them. When that mother bear came back to shore with the seal kill, in that short period of time, the cub had learned an invaluable lesson in how to hunt without the benefit of an ice pan. A lesson in survival to be passed on and on.

This was not the only occasion I witnessed behavior that left me scratching my head and marveling at these amazing hunters. During the summer months, my town hosts another animal gathering that is just as exciting and spectacular as the polar bears in fall. Each June through August, a few thousand beluga whales come through to feed, mate, and give birth in the warm freshwater of the Churchill River. At the same time, polar bears that have come off a long winter and spring hunt can be found cooling off in backwater pools along the riverbank or floating with the changing tides that reach almost ten miles (sixteen kilometers) upstream.

One summer towards the end of July, I was out on the riverbank a few miles from where it drains into Hudson Bay. It's a rare day in Churchill when you can sit beside the river on a warm summer afternoon enjoying a cold beverage with a friend, mesmerized by the sun sparkling off the calm waters of a slow flood tide. The river's glassy surface was broken here and there by hundreds of beluga whales breaching quietly while making their way upstream. The sight was both hypnotic and healing. It was almost too much for a couple of old hell-raisers like my friend Greg and me, but soon an event out in the middle of the river caught our eye and snapped us to attention. Something was thrashing about causing a commotion amongst the whales. Enough of a commotion to get us up and into the Zodiac to check it out.

Motoring towards where we last saw the plumes of water flying up, we searched for the cause but couldn't see anything. The river was calm and the whales continued on their lazy way, but something was not quite in sync with everything else. It looked like a patch of off-white foam floating slowly from side to side. We cut way back on the throttle and eased our way towards it. An old polar bear was floating flat out and face down, like a Hugh Hefner rug, using his back legs as a rudder to alter his direction within the tide flow. We held off a ways before following.

There were whales breaching all around the old bear, and our boat as well, when the old guy saw an opportunity and tried to grab an unsuspecting beluga as it rose to the top for air. He had a hold of it for a short while, the water boiling with the tussle, but the whale got away. The bear flattened out and continued hunting.

It wasn't long before the calm waters burst with another attempt by the bear. This time he got lucky. We watched him grab a smaller whale in a huge hug and quickly bite down hard on its head. It didn't take long for the whale to stop struggling. Everything was calm within a few minutes, like nothing happened. The bear released his grip on the whale's head, slid down the length of his catch, and grabbed the tail in his mouth.

We decided to follow the successful hunter and his trophy as he slowly made his way across the water to a patch of willows hugging the riverbank. We watched as he hauled the whale out of the water and

around the edge of the willows into a shallow bay. If the spectacle of the old guy hunting wasn't enough, we were floored by what we saw next. There, hidden in the small bay, were two more polar bears. They looked younger than the hunter and a little smaller. Beside them, half-hidden in the willows, was a second dead whale that the trio had been feeding off. All three bears were watching us, but they showed no alarm or discomfort. If anything, we felt a little bad for intruding. We backed off and let them be.

It was a quiet day in late October when I saw him approaching from the east. He appeared small in the binoculars, taking forever with his slow plodding but never wavering from the track he set. As he drew closer, I could see he was an old warrior heavily scarred with patches of black skin where thick underfur had been. His once-great white coat was now yellowed with age. I love these old bears. All banged up from a lifetime of struggle, they live mostly on wits and lessons learned, each face with a thousand stories.

The bear grew suspicious of my presence the closer he got and was still quite a ways off when he stopped walking. I had parked the camera buggy along the coast, and it looked to me that I was in his way. He just stood there watching, his tired eyes fixed on the buggy. After an unreasonable length of time, I got the message. I started the buggy, put it in reverse, and backed away from the old bear's set track. In a few minutes he continued on his way, eventually crossing where I was parked, passing without so much as a sideways glance.

The bear didn't get far. Along the coast, a short distance from where I sat, was a shallow bay rimmed with stands of reddish dwarf willow. It was less than a bay, more an indent really, a break in the coastline where seawater got trapped in a pool after a high tide. The old guy stopped at a small flat area on a raised hummock partially hidden by the willows but close to the mouth of the break.

Like all tidal waters, Hudson Bay is influenced by the gravitational pull of the moon. The bay's average high tide may be thirteen feet (four meters), but around the time of a full moon, with a corresponding strong north wind pushing the water, the tides can become as high as sixteen feet (five meters) or more. When the tides are that large, the water will breach the tidal ridge and flood behind it. Depending on the severity of the storm, the flooding can be quite extensive, especially in these low-lying areas. In hindsight, the old bear's timing was good.

The next day broke miserably with a hard north wind, heavy overcast skies, and driving rain. Not unusual weather for the end of October in these northern climes, but with a full moon coming this was the perfect buildup to a raging storm. The old bear hadn't moved since his arrival the day before and sat watching and waiting. I made the mistake of trying to get closer to see what he was up to and he moved away. The old guy didn't need me bothering him, so I drove to a place further up the coast but still close enough that I could see what was going on. In a short time he returned to his resting spot.

The coast was being battered by the wind and sea, the highest tide of the month was on the rise, and the moon was full. The wind rocked the camera buggy something fierce, and sleep did not come easily if at all.

The storm let up during the night and in the morning I saw the extent of the flooding. The water had reached far inland and formed shallow lakes behind the tidal ridges. The old bear was still at his spot—his little rise of earth was now almost an island. As the mass of water that was forced inland was receding, I caught a sudden movement out of the corner of my eye. A flash of white. A splash of water. With a speed and ferocity that you would not expect from a beat-up old man, the bear had a young seal by the back of the neck raised high out of the water. I could barely contain myself and let out a big whoop. The old bugger got one. Every now and then for the rest of the day, the bear would raise his head over top of the willows to look in my direction. The red on his snout seemed out of place on such a regal face.

In the morning the old guy was gone. The chance to get on the ground and have a look at where he'd spent the last few days presented itself, and so I took it. There was no seal carcass. All I found was a smudge of blood on a rock. The remains of the huge body of water brought in by the high tide was draining back to the sea funneled through the narrow break in the beach ridge. This break, now seen from the bear's perspective, was further restricted by a corridor of large rocks extending from the edge of the break toward the center. The rocks would have guided anything caught in the large tide pool along the narrow opening back to the sea. Including seals. It was quite a revelation. The old guy had it all figured out—right down to the high tide and full moon. It was all too slick to be coincidental. He knew this place, and there was no doubt in my mind that he had had success here in the past.

You cannot underestimate the intelligence of polar bears. The more I am around them, the more I am convinced that their ingenuity will see them through the hardest of times. Their innate knowledge of the unique habitat they live in secures their future—only if we do our part not to screw it up.

deniers

A few years back, I was surprised to find my name on a list of people who did not believe that manmade global warming was a legitimate issue. I was labeled a denier. I found it a bit bizarre, as I didn't recall ever talking to anyone in any depth about climate change. Yet there I was, listed between biologist Josef Reichholf, Head of Vertebrates Department of the National Zoological Collection in Munich, and evolutionary biologist and paleozoologist Dr. Susan Crockford. Good company.

I had a good laugh, followed by worry and slight nausea, wondering who the jerk was that put the list together. Boy, did he make a big mistake. Until I read on and discovered it wasn't a mistake. Not exactly. After my name there was a quote from a conversation I had with David Jones, a journalist for a well-read British newspaper. I suppose this quote, taken out of context, was all that was needed to include me on a list that would be looked down on by the masses. Questioning the effects of climate change has connotations akin to denying the Holocaust.

I met David in 2007 when he came over from England at the request of fellow countryman Nigel Marven, a TV producer and presenter, to write an article about *Polar Bear Week*, a made-for-television documentary series Nigel was in the midst of shooting. I had worked with Nigel previously on other projects about polar bears and was hired on to do this five-part series filming throughout the Canadian Arctic with a big chunk shot in and around Churchill. While David wrote his piece, he was handed over to me to look after so he wasn't eaten by a bear.

We were set up on the edge of a frozen lake, a bit closer than we should have been, near two big males that had just finished a serious round of sparring. They had put on quite the performance and were now lying belly down in newly fallen snow to cool off. Everyone agreed this sequence of battling polar bears was just what was needed for the show. Although I've found that wildlife filmmakers are never fully satisfied with what they shoot, this was as good as it gets.

David made a comment about how robust and healthy the bears looked given the fact that this group was reportedly on the brink of starvation. What he saw didn't fit the image of what he had expected to see. The two bears were obviously nowhere near starvation. In fact, during the time he was here he never saw a polar bear that looked anything like what was being depicted in the media. What was that all about?

My answer to the question was simple: the Churchill polar bears were not starving to death. They were suffering at the hands of spin-doctors who were making this iconic animal the sad face of doom to further a myriad of agendas that feed off the bears' prescribed extinction. In other words, it was all lies.

Spending the little time he did with me, I am sure David quickly concluded that I was no scholar. Not even close. But he did know I had the benefit of observing and working closely with this group of bears for almost thirty years. My experience with these animals offers insight that most do not have.

In the past, even though I was seeing healthy polar bears, I asked myself if the experts were seeing something I wasn't. Yes, I had heard the predictions of an ice-free Arctic taking away their ability to hunt seal. Yes, there was a change in weather patterns. Yes, freeze-up was taking a bit longer in the fall, lengthening the wait time for bears to get out on the ice. And yet, it appeared the bears were doing fine. What was I missing?

It became clear when I watched a live webcast by a conservation organization that has positioned itself as the eminent authority on polar bears. It is the organization most people, including journalists, reference when seeking information. It was broadcast from a Tundra Buggy parked along the coast east of Churchill. There were three well-known polar bear biologists sitting up front facing the camera. The occasional polar bear passed by the window behind them. Someone off-camera was asking scripted questions. The theme throughout the webcast was how mankind's excess was destroying the planet. "Reducing your carbon footprint" was a reoccurring catch phrase. At one point, a scientist was prompted to make a comment. With all the drama he could muster, he looked woefully out the window and said that in all the years he had been coming here he had never seen the bears so weak and skinny, so lethargic. It was obvious to him that they were starving, global warming had caught up with them, and it was too late. The other two bobbleheads nodded in agreement. I was watching from my own truck, looking at the same group of bears, and couldn't believe what I was hearing. Did this guy really want people to believe these bears were dying of starvation right before our eyes?

The day of the webcast was miserable with heavy skies and freezing rain. Bears were hunkered down in the kelp beds, some back in the willows, and a few trudged around close to my truck. Polar bears, like humans, do not like playing around in weather like this. The day before the webcast was cold and sunny. Fresh snow softened the frozen ground and bouts of sparring were popping up all along the coast. Bears were excited and moving around as the hunt was fast approaching and they could taste it in the air. The day after the webcast, once the bad weather passed, the bears shook it off and came to life again. These were the bears I had been looking at for years. Nothing had changed. The bears were very much alive. The experts were dead wrong.

Admittedly, I always gave science and researchers the benefit of the doubt. I believed they were fighting the good fight. Now I am not so sure. The remark made in the webcast concerning the state of these animals was either by a guy who did not have a clue about polar bear behavior or it was purposefully misleading. The fact that all three biologists were in agreement led me to believe it was a carefully scripted and staged lie.

This was troublesome. How does an average person make an informed decision about the well-being of our planet, and its inhabitants, if the information given is bogus? He can't. How does the average Joe know if the information he is given is true? He doesn't. When the information is coming from a high-profile organization, who would doubt the validity of what is said or presented? Not many. So, who was listening?

Of course, the journalists were listening—nothing like the impending extinction of a species to spice up the front page. But what was most disturbing was that this webcast was being streamed live into classrooms all over North America. There were hundreds, if not thousands, of impressionable kids gathered watching wild polar bears and listening to what these biologists had to say about their fate.

To present to children the specter of starving polar bears with little to no chance of survival seemed cruel. To burden them with the thought they were in some way responsible seemed wrong. That a trusted organization, listed as a charity in Canada, would offer school children anything less than the truth does not sit well with me. If the truth did not help the organization push their agenda forward, at least they could have offered hope. How unfortunate both were absent.

So what had I said that placed me on a government list of climate debunkers? I told David that journalists and photographers and filmmakers were coming to Churchill to document starving polar bears. They were doing so because organizations like that one had repeatedly announced the Churchill bears were on the brink of extinction. But when they got here they were confused, just as he was.

I said the bears I was looking at were the same bears I had been looking at for the last twenty-five years, some years better than others, but, on the whole, they remained healthy. I also said I hadn't noticed a marked decline in the number of bears. The population looked stable to me. My words were published by his newspaper and later picked up by the United States Senate committee who compiled the list. My observations were taken as something a person who denies the existence of a rapidly changing climate would say. Except I never spoke of climate change in that article.

A prominent conservation group once came across a mother polar bear that was very sick and unable to feed her two cubs, both near death from starvation. Over a period of three days, they filmed this family group. The video showed one young cub wracked with convulsions. It eventually died. The footage was sent to the Cancun Climate Summit in 2010, not as an example of polar bears dying from the effects of climate change but to share what a polar bear would look like *if* it were to die of starvation due to climate change. It sent a message that, in my mind, was loud and clear: the immediate well being of these animals was not the main priority. The value was not in rescuing the starving cubs but in documenting their suffering.

As long as we don't save them to death, these polar bears are handling whatever Mother Nature throws at them. It is what human beings throw at them that will be their downfall. I do not deny that extremes in the weather are causing additional burdens on this group of bears, but I do not buy into the hysteria over their inevitable extinction prophesied by organizations that have agendas other than the immediate well-being of the Churchill polar bears.

No group of bears on the planet has been subjected to the assault this group has endured for the past thirty years. The risk of being chased by helicopter and shot with a tranquillizer dart is something these bears face from the day they are born until the day they die. The process once they are "down" is degrading. They are shaved, milked, tagged, tattooed, and painted. The single most traumatic experience a mother with newborn cubs is faced with, beyond natural occurrences, is what they might be put through in the name of science. This method of collecting information is not without other dangers. The eight-inch dart can, and does, miss the mark sometimes, ending up embedded in a bear's stomach causing serious injury or death. Heat exhaustion, drowning, and broken legs from trying to escape the helicopter are all real injuries sustained by these bears. I wonder when the trauma and pain the animal has to endure will become more important than the collection of data. If the Churchill bears are near extinction because of the stresses of a rapidly changing climate, wouldn't you think adding to that stress would reduce any chance of them coping and adapting to stay alive? Progress made in the name of science is not always justifiable. Perhaps if we leave the bears alone, they'll adapt on their own terms. If there's a list for that, feel free to add me.

Mother Nature is tricky. —D.C.

denning

It was going on the end of November with six days left in the Cape Churchill tour. We came across a mother with two cubs of the year. She was an experienced mom, you could tell by her calm demeanor and the fact she still carried a bit of weight after a long summer and fall. She had managed her resources well.

We noticed the difference in size of the cubs but weren't alarmed by it. It isn't unheard of for one cub to be slightly bigger than the other. The family was a few miles along the coast heading towards the big tower and wasn't bothered by us following alongside at a respectful distance. When the big cub was hungry and nudged his mother behind her front legs, she stopped and gathered her cubs in to nurse.

As a guide for professional photographers and filmmakers, a nursing sequence can be the highlight of the day. It is humbling when the mother doesn't find us a threat and feels safe with us close by during her most vulnerable moments.

When it was time to continue on, the small cub had a hard time getting to its feet. Once it did, a small spot of blood was left on the snow. Mom was on her way but had stopped and waited for the little one to catch up. It became clear the little one was sickly. The cub was slow to get started and found difficulty keeping up. There were no outwardly visible signs of injury, so I knew that whatever was going on was internal.

The days are short that time of the year and by mid-afternoon, with daylight slipping away in the west, we left the family nestled together in deep snow caught by a patch of willow. The decision was made to try to find the family in the morning to see how things were going.

We returned to the spot where we left them to find an empty bed and telltale drops of red leading towards the cape. We worried about the little guy. They would soon find themselves in amongst a dozen or so big hungry males milling about waiting for the final push out onto the ice to hunt.

The scene we came across next was heartbreaking. The little guy couldn't get up. His mother and the larger cub were way ahead, occasionally looking back. It was tough love, but the threat of leaving him behind had to work. He found the strength to get to his feet and, in a series of stops and starts, slowly caught up. Mom would allow him a short rest before she started again. The bigger cub wanted to roughhouse but to no avail. The little guy was exhausted.

Up until this point, we thought the mother bear could have easily left the sick cub to die and continued on with the healthy one. We knew that the little one was going to be a burden. Even if it somehow made it onto the ice, it would seriously restrict the mother's ability to hunt, putting all of their lives at risk. It was assumed that these big animals could thoughtlessly give up on one their offspring to assure safe passage of another.

We were wrong. What transpired over the next few days left us in awe of the deep commitment this mom had towards her ailing cub. The emotional gauntlet she went through, and what it took us through as helpless observers, changed the way we felt about these remarkable animals. I knew then that these beasts had great capacity for grief and caring and for life.

The family made it and found a spot on a little rise giving the mother a clear view of the long sweep of beach rimming the cape and of the waiting bears dotting the coastline. But they didn't arrive unnoticed.

The final trek left the little cub completely drained. His rear end, now matted with blood, was visible from any angle. He wouldn't get up again. Night came. We stayed and the assaults started.

For the next two days, big male bears challenged the mom to get to the dying cub. The ferocity with which the cub was protected, not only from the mother but also by the other cub, kept the aggressors at bay. When given a reprieve from the onslaught, she would nurse the healthy one and nudge and pull at the sickly one trying to get him to respond. The bigger cub often lay on top or tightly alongside being as close as he could for comfort. The mother tried pulling the little one forward by the ear but couldn't move him because he was frozen to the ground. And the bears kept coming.

We stayed long into the first night feeling helpless and saddened by what was unfolding in front of us. The little one had died. The mother's grief was palpable and revealed itself in low, guttural cries of anguish. Her rage against the oncoming bears couldn't be sustained. She was now protecting the body. At one point she dug into the frozen ground trying to get underneath it to break it free of the ice but she tired quickly.

The dead cub was drawing bears from all sides. Exhaustion was setting in but the mother never gave up and wouldn't hesitate to jump on the backs of a retreating bear that got too close. It was getting to the point where the big cub couldn't be nursed while close to the body. A choice had to be made. She went a distance away to feed her remaining cub.

The first few times, she rushed back to drive away the bears that saw an opportunity to grab the cub and run, but the cub was frozen to the ground and couldn't be moved. Those bears quickly felt the fury of an enraged mother.

The emotional wave we all were carried away on had us beat as night fell again. The mother had a deep gash along her shoulder and was fading quickly. Her remaining cub was bewildered and needed rest. From inside the buggy we watched as a huge male approached the cub. We waited for the mother to come out of the dark. The big male claimed the prize with no one around to challenge him.

The prevailing north winds carry snow across the barren land until it is caught and held by stands of dwarf willow. This hearty shrub can be found around the edges of small, shallow lakes and streams and is common and plentiful where the boreal forest gives way to the Hudson Bay Lowlands, an ideal habitat to support one of the largest populations of polar bears birthing cubs. The snow that builds on the lee side of these willows offers the perfect cover and insulation for the earth dens used by generations of female bears. Some of these dens are ancient.

In early March 1996, my partner and I were traveling along the northern edge of a narrow lake about forty-three miles (seventy kilometers) south of Churchill looking for active bear dens for a documentary filmmaker. One of the great thrills for anyone who enjoys nature is watching newborn polar bear cubs emerge from the maternal den for the first time. It's an incredible sight never to be forgotten. We knew we were in the right place but worried about the timing.

What caught our eye was a small circular break in the surface of a long drift of snow leading down from the base of a willow patch. It would have been easy to miss. We were cautiously excited as this could indicate that a mother recently broke through the bank of snow covering the entrance to her den. There were no disturbances other than the hole, which gave us hope that there was a new family under there ready to come out. We decided that I would stay to watch and see if the mother would show herself, or if there was anything to see at all. My partner would continue looking for other potentially active dens.

The sun was a few hours old, still low in the eastern sky, offering a false promise of relief from the numbing cold. March is not a good month to be hanging around outside waiting for something to happen. I didn't want to cause a ruckus, and I tried to be as still as I could, but you have to move around in that weather. The cold worked its way through my heavy winter parka in no time at all, and I soon found myself forcing back the shivers.

My mind wandered as I waited. How many cubs did she have? Did they survive? Would she show herself soon? Some bears have no problem with humans at a distance, but others will not tolerate them, which one was she?

Answers came quickly. In a matter of minutes, her head popped out and, without hesitation, she hauled herself out and slid down the short bank of snow to the frozen lake, her fur tinged yellow from the months spent in the den. She was relishing the freedom, rolling and rubbing her great coat on the ice and snow. As fascinated as I was by her behavior, I wondered about the possible cubs. You had to look hard, but just over the rim of the hole you could see two sets of coal-black eyes intensely focused on their mother. A pair of brand new polar bears.

Mother Nature is tricky. Once she has your attention she can evoke feelings so profound that they can cause the knees of a rough-and-ready guy like me to shake. A certain grace washed over me while watching the cubs tumble out of the den down to where their mother was laying. Caught up in the joy of the moment, it was easy to forget the overwhelming struggle that mother would face in the weeks and months to come.

After viewing the young family for nearly a week, as the mother bear allowed the cubs to gain strength outside the den, I watched as she led them on the long walk to the frozen sea. The sunlight got caught in their fur. As the mother set a determined pace, trailing wisps of breath remained visible in the chilled air. It was a beautiful morning.

Dancer was no ordinary bear.
D.C.

about a bear

My hometown is ground zero in the fight to save the polar bears. Of the nineteen populations of polar bears identified worldwide, the bears of Churchill are being singled out as the first that will disappear from the face of the earth in just fifteen to twenty years. It is a hard pill to swallow considering how intelligent and resourceful these bears are, and it will take more than the extrapolation of selective data to convince me.

I received an email from David Jones, the journalist I'd met a few years before on a shoot with Nigel Marven. The tone of the message seemed urgent. I was given a phone number and asked to please call as soon as I could, regardless of the time in Canada or in the United Kingdom.

We spent ten days together on Nigel's shoot. All of the bear sequences were filmed on the ground and, whenever possible, close to the action. Nigel was pleased. The final two days were going to be filmed from a Tundra Buggy at Gordon Point. It had been a few years since I quit operating the Polar Bear Cam. When I did, I lost access to that area and gave up being with Dancer for the few weeks we visited each year. In the end, not being able to see the old bear was really the only thing I regretted about the whole situation. I hadn't been back in a few years and was very much looking forward to it. I really wanted to see if he still came back and how he was doing—I wanted to know if he was still alive.

Not getting my hopes up of finding my old pal didn't stop me from trying to spot him. We bounced around the area, filming when we could off the back of the buggy where there was a nice open deck. It was a long day and everyone was enjoying themselves, but collectively we were tired and all talked out. Quietly sitting back in our seats, lulled by the swaying of the big buggy, I spotted him far out on the ice making his way north. He looked as if he was heading out to begin the hunt. Dancer has a distinctive walk noticeable at any distance. It was him alright.

The moment felt personal to me. I wasn't sure if I wanted, or needed, to share it with everyone else on the buggy. I could have just watched him amble along over the frozen sea without the others knowing.

Nigel knew about Dancer. I had talked about him enough over the last week or so. But I don't know if he believed everything I said. In fact, that was the problem surrounding my friendship with this bear. Everyone wanted to see me with Dancer.

I thought back to when we first met, almost twenty years before at Cape Churchill. He was just a young cub trailing behind his mother and twin brother when I saw him. What made him noticeably different than other cubs I have seen was his independence and fearless curiosity. He just wouldn't listen to his mother. There was a degree of intelligence emanating from the little bear that one could not miss. I started playing a game with him. Once I got his attention I would duck down below the deck wall, so he couldn't see me, and then pop up in a different spot to surprise him. It was as much fun for me as for him. The family group stuck around where we were camped at the cape until it was time for us to go. I had a chance to play this game with him every day we were there. He started to stand up on his hind legs and walk backwards trying to see me when I dropped out of sight on the back deck. He looked like a wobbly line dancer when he did this. Dancer was a good name for him.

Fast track years later to when I was living in old Buggy One along the Hudson Bay coast operating the Polar Bear Cam. He came up to the buggy and pushed against the side so hard it had me worried I was under attack. When the big bear and I saw each other through the window, he immediately reared up on his hind legs and took a few wobbly few steps backwards. Dancer had found me.

He was the featured guest on the Polar Bear Cam and his antics entertained people worldwide. Our relationship was a big part of my daily diary that I wrote and posted on the website. Each fall, I couldn't wait to get the buggy out on the coast, start up the camera, and wait for my pal to find me, which he always did around November the fourth every year I was there.

He loved the smells coming from inside the buggy and he learned how to gently open the sliding window on the driver's door with the tip of his giant claw. He would stick his head in for a visit and fill his senses with all that was going on inside. I would scratch him behind his ear.

He was a gentle bear and if I offered a treat, which I did sparingly, he would take it from me without the slightest hint of being anything but grateful. He received food but never begged—it was not his style.

He didn't like the attention he was getting from the touring buggies. They would park beside us, too close to his spot below my driver's door window. He increasingly became one of the most sought after bears to photograph. I was constantly asked to have him stand up at my window and scratch his nose and make him dance. He didn't like being made a fool of, and I didn't like playing the fool by doing it.

So, I was reluctant to call him when I spotted him far out on the ice. I didn't want to make him dance for anyone anymore.

I thought back to one long, dark night sitting alone in Buggy One, my mind and body numbed by melancholy, when a light scrape of metal and a tickle of cold air turned my head towards Dancer's window. He had slid it open and was silently watching me, not moving or making a sound, careful of my emotions.

We grew old together. The memories of the years I spent waiting for Dancer are a bittersweet time for me now knowing he might not be around much longer.

And then it just blurted out of me. "Nigel, get the camera ready. You're in for a treat." I needed to see him up close, maybe for the last time. I wanted to see if he would respond to me, if he wanted to visit.

The guys on the buggy didn't know what I was talking about but the camera operator got the camera out, the sound guy readied the recorder, and Nigel asked a thousand questions. I pointed to the bear far out on the ice and told him it was my pal Dancer and I was going to call him. I wanted them to get it on film.

Dancer recognized my voice and turned his head towards the buggy, paused for a second, then altered his course and came towards me. I was ecstatic. I didn't hear any of the commotion going on in the buggy with the crew and everyone else jockeying for positions at the windows and back deck. He came up to the buggy but he was cautious. It wasn't Buggy One he was approaching, but he knew my voice. He lay down under the driver's window and looked up at me. He had a few more scars and looked older, but it was the same funny and gentle bear that made me laugh and wonder for all those years. The others made him visibly nervous, so I asked them to move away from the windows and to be as quiet as they could be. In a moment or two, after everyone settled, the big bear reared up on his hind legs, placing his plate-sized mitts against the side of the buggy, and stuck his head towards me to get his nose scratched.

The connection I had with Dancer was why David Jones sent the urgent message to call. He was writing an article on Thomas Dörflein, who worked for the Berlin Zoo as the keeper of a polar bear cub named Knut. This darling of a bear was rejected at birth by his mother and had to be raised by hand. Thomas took up the task and spent most of his time doing just that. They were inseparable for the next two years and became celebrities. In the summer of 2008, the zoo decided it was too dangerous to allow Thomas in such close quarters with the growing bear, even though he'd raised Knut from birth. Thomas died suddenly two months later (as would Knut in 2011).

The journalist asked for a comment from me thinking I might offer insight into how deep a relationship there could be between a man and a bear. The spin being that the connection the two had was so strong that Thomas lost his will to live once removed from Knut's daily life. Makes for a heart-wrenching story.

> *He had a few more scars and looked older, but it was the same funny and gentle bear that made me laugh and wonder for all those years.* —D.C.

Upwind of Dancer as he lay in the snow one day, Dennis leaned out the window of our truck and let out the call he had used over the last twenty years: "Here Dancer, c'mon boy. C'mon Dancer!" Immediately and with obvious recognition, the big bear looked our way and was up and coming at a dead run through the lime grass. He stopped about twenty feet from the truck and Dennis talked to him for five minutes—just two old guys reconnecting on the shore of Hudson Bay. /A.B.

There is a difference between developing a relationship with a captive-born polar bear that relies on you for everything and a wild polar bear that relies on you for nothing. One begins out of necessity, the other out of curiosity. There was a lot of emotion on my part each year as I waited to see my pal again and, given the intelligence of these bears, I would like to think Dancer was happy when he saw me. But I am reluctant to take it further than that. Still, the encounter I had with Dancer that day after not seeing him for a few years is a memory I will never forget.

In the years since, I have seen him and kept my distance most of the time. But not all the time. If no one was around, I would still call him over for a one-on-one chat.

Dancer was no ordinary bear — D.C.

Dennis and Dancer / 2004

Dennis and Dancer / 2005

I hope he's still out there.

D.C.

photog

As the sun dropped to the horizon, the mother moved her charges to the top of the snow bank, and it looked like we had taken our last pics of the day. But suddenly, in a burst of vibrant yellow, sunlight shot from beneath the band of clouds hugging the horizon. At almost the same time, the mother reversed course and headed back down the snowbank, parading her babies past us, obviously very proud to show them off. Then she headed up the bank, with the two cubs struggling behind, stopped, turned to pose one last time, and was gone. The entire sequence lasted less than 30 seconds, but it was one of those rare but magical moments that makes being with wild animals so rewarding. /A.B.

A strong north wind started to build ice and pack it against various outcroppings of land along the coast. This loosely packed ice is a pretty stable platform for a bear, and the mother most likely took her cub there to stay away from the threat of a male bear. After some time, the tide and the wind reversed and the ice started to pull apart. What ensued was a magical fifteen minutes as the mother and cub methodically worked their way back to shore – zigging and zagging to find the best route, jumping from one ice block to another, and occasionally falling in before finally making it to shore. /A.B.

WAITING FOR DANCER

A two-year old cub climbed up to where I was shooting from the roof hatch of my Suburban, Big Red. I talked to him for about ten minutes before his mom barked at him and he went running. /A.B.

At times it seems as though wild animals, when they are accustomed to you and have accepted you as being nonthreatening, start to realize that you are there because you have an interest in them. And in those cases, it almost seems like they start posing for the camera. This was one of those moments. /A.B.

A mother and her pair of two-year-old cubs out on the ice. The young male is testing his boundaries. These cubs will be on their own in six months and the mother wants them to learn to be independent. /A.B.

This was the first photograph that I ever took of a polar bear–a young female roaming around the Great White Bear Tundra Lodge in November 2008. /A.B.

Polar bears can spar like this for days—and often do. Funny thing is, nobody ever gets hurt. Maybe you will see an accidental spot of blood but not often. Doing this helps kill time while waiting for freeze-up and also helps them build strength and fighting skills that they will need while out on the ice—either to fight for food or for mates. /A.B.

130

WAITING FOR DANCER

WAITING FOR DANCER

WAITING FOR DANCER

In near whiteout conditions, we were on the ground trying to get close to this bear. Two other bears were lurking just out of sight, which made it ideal conditions for an ambush attack. One rushed us and only stopped when Dennis chambered a round in his shotgun. /A.B.

acknowledgements

ANDREW BAZELEY

Morris & Mike Spence of Wat'chee Lodge in the Wapusk National Park, one of the few places on earth to see mothers coming out of the den with their cubs.

Denise Earle of the Traveller's Touchstone B&B in Churchill – great hostess of the best B&B around.

Brian Ladoon, who facilitated lots of great bear viewing at his Canadian Husky kennels.

Lawreen & Mike Spence, owners of the Seaport Hotel, for their hospitality and for providing the watering hole where I first met Dennis.

The Canadian Legion Hall and all of its patrons – spent many a fun evening there drinking beers with the guys.

Kal Barteski for her friendship, her passion for this book, and for her artistic genius.

Alexandra Asher Sears for her commitment to us and the book and her incredible skill as a wordsmith.

Dennis Compayre – best bear guide ever and a damned good friend.

My children, Landon and Brittany Bazeley, for their love and for their support.

And last but not least, my Golden Retriever, Buzz Lightyear, my best buddy.

- A.B.

DENNIS COMPAYRE

My hometown, Churchill on Hudson Bay, and all who inhabit it, past and present, on four legs and two.

Joanne and the boys: Kelsey, Joe, Murray, Lonnie, and young Johnny Utah.

Tony, Leslie, and Lorne Compayre.

Thanks to Esther and Debbie.

Good ol' boys: Beef, Hammy, Chris, Albert, Wayne, Jack, Kelsey, and Greg.

Associates at the big table, Churchill Legion.

Associates at the little table, Seaport Hotel.

Len and Bev Smith.

Merv, Lynda, and John Gunter…for the chance.

Boris and Helen.

Paul Clifford, Tom Mangelsen, and Nigel Marven.

A nod to my polar bear brothers: Paul, Morris, Mike, Brian, Umuk, and Wally.

Kal and Alex…for believing.

And my friend Andrew…thanks.

C'mon, Dancer!

- D.C.